D1527444

Library of Congress Control Number
In progress
ISBN: 9798359260152

This book is dedicated to all those who called Harris Neck home and those who have fought to have their homeland returned to them.

FOREWORD

I would like to thank Harry and Dave for having the courage to write this book. Harry has had first-hand knowledge of how the people in our government have treated us, the people of Harris Neck.

How our way of like was destroyed and left us wanting. Our culture in shambles and most of our elders dying or hopeless. My grandfather's shrimp boat rotted on the bank of the river, just as the other family boats. No oysters, shrimp or fish. Crops in the fields taken or destroyed. Homes demolished or burned down.

I am amazed at how mentally strong some of them were. Trauma can kill you too. I have learned from them, from their experience of what happened to them. I have the courage to fight on. I am not bitter or hateful. We have been wronged.

I still have hope that my government will do the right thing and return our land to us. Thanks, Harry and Dave for exposing an ugly truth. The hate some of us are still living under. Slavery, segregation and Jim Crow. We are still standing and I will stand come what may.

Wilson Moran
Harris Neck Descendant
Fall 2022

CONTENTS

Chapter 4: War Comes to Harris Neck

E. M. Thorpe
Fifth Amendment to Constitution
Federal Promise Made
Harris Neck Army Airbase
Surplus Property Act

Chapter 5: Poppell's Playground

Poppell Dynasty
U. S. 17
Harris Neck Refuge
60 Minutes Show
GAO Report

Chapter 6: Seeking A Solution

Harris Neck Justice Movement
People Organized for Equal Rights
Federal Court Cases
Congressional Hearing
Army Acquisition Data

Chapter 7: Birth of Harris Neck Land Trust

National Public Radio

Prologue:

On January 3, 2015, I retired from the U. S. House of Representatives. I had spent nearly 38 years working as a staffer for our nation's highest legislative body. This experience was the greatest honor of my life.

During the last 20 years of my Capitol Hill career, I served as the Republican Staff Director of the Committee on Natural Resources Subcommittee on Fisheries, Wildlife, Oceans and Insular Affairs. I was provided with both administrative and policy staff. These professionals were experts on the issues before the Subcommittee.

During those two decades, Republicans were the majority party for 16 of the 20 years. As the majority party, we scheduled public hearings, decided which bills would be moved through the legislative process, and controlled the policy agenda. My Subcommittee Chairmen during this period were Congressmen James Saxton of Mount Holly, New Jersey, Wayne T. Gilchrist of

Kennedyville, Maryland and Dr. John
Fleming of Minden, Louisiana.

One of my jobs as Staff Director was
to review the hundreds of letters written
to my Subcommittee Chairmen. Most of
these missives were member of Congress
requests asking for a hearing on a specific
bill or subject matter. I carefully
examined each letter and would
recommend certain ones.

Our Subcommittee was always
extremely busy and there was neither the
time nor interest in honoring each
request. Over the course of eight
Congresses, my Subcommittee conducted
278 Congressional hearings. This
included 135 oversight hearings on
federal agency budgets, governmental
programs under our jurisdiction and
miscellaneous topics. The net result of our
efforts was the enactment of 143 new
federal laws.

Over the course of these 20 years,
there were a handful of hearings that
deeply affected me. One of those hearings
had been requested by Congressman Jack
Kingston of Savannah, Georgia. In his

letter, he asked Dr. Fleming to conduct an oversight hearing on the Harris Neck community in McIntosh County that was part of his 1st Congressional District.

I remember reading his letter. I had never heard of Harris Neck, Georgia and how it became a national wildlife refuge in 1962. Nevertheless, I had spent nearly 30 years working on issues, problems and legislation affecting the National Wildlife Refuge System.

In fact, I had visited a number of wildlife refuges including the neighboring Okefenokee National Wildlife Refuge in Georgia. I had been the lead Republican staffer responsible for the drafting of the historic National Wildlife Refuge System Improvement Act of 1997. The author of this law was my boss Chairman Don Young of Alaska.

Before meeting with Dr. Fleming, I did some research. I was shocked to learn that the majority of the 2,687 acres designated as refuge lands had once been owned by former Georgia slaves. It had been legally willed to a former slave Robert Delegall on September 2, 1865 by his former plantation owner Margret Ann Harris of Harris Neck, Georgia.

What I conveyed to Dr. Fleming was that between 1865 and 1942, four generations of former slaves and their descendants engaged in subsistence farming, crabbing, fishing and oystering on the land and waters of Harris Neck. I also told him that in 1942 the U.S. Department of War was seeking sites in coastal Georgia to construct airfields to train army combat pilots. War Department officials met with the political leaders of McIntosh County, Georgia. While there were numerous potential sites, county leaders persuaded the federal officials to select the 2,687 acres of Harris Neck for the Army airfield.

There was nothing special about the site except that the overwhelming majority of the landowners were African Americans. The War Department cruelly used their eminent domain power to condemn and confiscate the property. It was a sad day in America.

Under the Fifth Amendment to our Constitution, the government must provide fair compensation for the taking of private property. In the case of Harris Neck, the government compensated property owners for their land but not their crops, equipment, homes or out-buildings. Legal records show that white property owners, who did not actually live on their land, received 40 percent more compensation for their land than black owners, all of whom lived in the thriving community known as Harris Neck. There was nothing fair or just about this flawed process.

The black community residents were given a few weeks to vacate their businesses and homes. On a dreary Monday, July 27th morning, federal bulldozers arrived to destroy the community's businesses, churches, homes, schoolhouse and one of their two cemeteries. Everything was then burned to the ground. Residents were forced to seek refuge in the adjacent pine forest. They put up tents or built lean-tos to protect them from the stifling summer heat. According to Mary Moran, they were "treated like animals."

As the rightful owners were leaving their sacred land, many of them received verbal promises by representatives of the federal government that when the Second World War was over they could get their land back. They are still waiting.

I also told Dr. Fleming that on December 7, 1979, the House Merchant Marine and Fisheries Committee held a hearing on H.R. 4018. Congressman Bo Ginn of Georgia, who represented the community, had introduced this bill. This legislation would have allowed the descendants of the Harris Neck property owners to repurchase their land at exactly the amount they were paid in 1943. Unfortunately, this bill did not advance through the legislative process.

After completing my briefing, Dr. Fleming agreed to the hearing. He contacted Congressman Jack Kingston. I was instructed to work with Mr. Kingston's office to define the focus of this hearing and to invite appropriate witnesses to testify. One of the first potential witnesses I spoke with was David M. Kelly the Project Coordinator for the Harris Neck Land Trust (Trust).

This organization was established in December of 2005. It represents the rightful heirs, black and white, to the 2,687 acres that were wrongly taken and later incorporated within the National Wildlife Refuge System.

On December 15, 2011, the Subcommittee on Fisheries, Wildlife, Oceans and Insular Affairs conducted the oversight hearing. For the first time in three decades, Congress got to hear the moving and troubling stories of Evelyn Greer, Wilson W. Moran, Winston Relaford, Sr. and Reverend Robert H. Thorpe. Evelyn Greer, was 15-years-old when the government burned down her home. In her testimony, she told the Committee, "We are here today not as beggars. We are here to see and ask you all to let justice prevail."

It is now ten years later. I still get emotional remembering their testimony. I am still angry that despite tremendous efforts by the Trust little has been accomplished. It is inconceivable and simply wrong that bipartisan administrations have failed to hear and act on their plea.

Despite a promise that the 2,687 acres would be returned to them after World War II, instead it became federal property. The Harris Neck National Wildlife Refuge was established in 1962. The members of the Trust simply want to celebrate their heritage by utilizing a portion of what their ancestors once proudly owned. I am confident in saying that of the more than 560 national wildlife refuges in this country, Harris Neck is the only refuge that contains land previously owned by those who were the victims of the abomination known as slavery.

For the past decade, I have stayed in contact with Dave Kelly. I have offered unsolicited advice. I have prepared Harris Neck briefing papers for my Capitol Hill contacts. I have visited the Harris Neck Wildlife Refuge, and in February 2020, I traveled to Atlanta, Georgia to meet with Fish and Wildlife Representatives at their Regional Office. They were kind to meet with a former legislative branch employee, and I remain hopeful that this meeting may eventually lead to a meaningful solution.

At the same time, Dave Kelly has worked tirelessly for the completion of a Cooperative Agreement, a land exchange or federal legislation to finally allow the long aggrieved people of Harris Neck to return to the land that is rightfully theirs. I am confident that this community will never give up its fight for justice.

During our relationship, Dave and I have discussed the possibility of writing a book about Harris Neck.

We believe the time has come to share this compelling story. In this book, we talk about the origins of Harris Neck, the 1865 "Will and Testament" of Margret Harris, what life was like for this community before and after World War II, the efforts of an organization known as the People Organized for Equal Rights, the two Congressional hearings, the birth of the Harris Neck Land Trust and how justice may finally be achieved for the descendants of those Americans who loved and nurtured this land so long ago.

We also provide a searing history of the horrible institution of slavery in the United States, how this isolated community on 2,87 acres existed within McIntosh County, Georgia, the Burning of Darien, Georgia, Sherman's March to the Sea and the heroic efforts of Abraham Lincoln to free 4 million long suffering African Americans. These are all interconnected events that have transpired over the last 300 years.

After more than 80 years of striving and waiting, it is time for justice. It is time for this nation to do the right thing. As President John F. Kennedy said, "If not now, when? If not by us, then by whom?

Chapter 1: Origins of Harris Neck

In 1736, William Harris (1720-1742) and his young bride Anne Coles ((1723-1759) left Scotland and emigrated to Savannah, Georgia. Their likely conveyance was the British frigate *The Prince of Wales.* Upon arriving in the Colony of Georgia, they hiked 62 miles south on the Northern Bank of the Altamaha River to the town of Darien, Georgia. This was the only Gaelic speaking community in Georgia.

Two years later, they had a son who they named William Thomas Harris (1738-1817). Like many of his Highland Scottish brethren, William Harris joined the army of the founder of the colony, James Edward Oglethorpe. Their mission was to protect the colonists and their property from the insidious raids of the Spanish Army.

Over a ten-year period, there had been numerous acts of piracy by British and Spanish forces. One of the most infamous occurred off the coast of Florida in April 1731. On that memorable day, Spanish privateers from the *La Isabella* boarded the HMS *Rebecca* under the command of British Captain Robert Jenkins. After a brief mock trial, Captain Jenkins was found guilty of raiding Spanish ships. Spanish Commander Juan de Leon Fandino used his cutlass to cut off the captain's left ear. After administering this punishment, he then graciously returned the ear to him.

According to legend, Captain Jenkins returned to England and presented his severed ear to the British House of Commons. It was preserved within a pickle jar. He then demanded retribution for his removed auricle and the British Parliament complied by approving the War of Jenkins Ear.

The decisive battle of this war occurred on July 17, 1742 on St. Simons Island, Georgia. The British forces at Fort Frederica were led by General James Oglethorpe. His army consisted of less than 1,000 regulars, local citizens, rangers and southeastern Native Americans. They were opposed by 2,000 well trained, heavily armed and battle tested Spanish ground troops. Their commander was the

Governor of Florida, General Don Manuel de Montiano.

It was called the Battle of Bloody Marsh because the marsh became red with the blood of Spanish soldiers. When the fighting stopped, nearly 200 Spanish troops had been killed. The rest of the army strategically retreated. They had simply run out of ammunition to fire their guns. By contrast, there were only a small number of casualties among members of Oglethorpe's army. One of those who died of his injuries was 22-year-old William Harris. The Spanish defeat at Bloody Marsh forever ended their dream of reclaiming their "Lost Colony" in Georgia.

With the passing of William Harris, his widow Anne Coles decided to remarry. Her second husband, Captain Daniel Demetre, was one of the original Scottish Highlander's and a member of Oglethorpe's army. He received land grants from the British Crown totaling about 240 acres in an area that would become known as Harris Neck. This area was comprised of extensive salt marshes, forested wetlands, freshwater ponds and mixed hardwood and pine trees.

During his life, Captain Demetre acquired hundreds of acres of property in McIntosh County, and he became wealthy because of his use of enslaved labor. Between 1750 and 1775, Georgia's slave population dramatically grew from less than 500 to 18,000 human beings. In 1757, Demetre died. Two years later, Anne Coles Harris Demetre joined him.

With their deaths, Anne's son, William Thomas Harris (1738-1786) inherited the Bethany Plantation and over 1,400 acres of property. In 1775, the *Georgia Gazette* called this land Harris Neck. William married Mary Elizabeth Landry (1738-1817). The couple had three sons. They were James Harris (1779-1804), William Thomas Harris, Jr. (1765-1825) and John Harris (1772-1827). All three sons were planters, who lived their entire lives on Harris Neck soil. Their three major cash crops were Sea Island cotton, indigo and Carolina Gold rice.

Upon the death of William Thomas Harris, Sr. in 1786, his oldest son and namesake took over the operation of the various enterprises on the Harris Neck plantation. Each of the three sons became rich men because African American men, women and children toiled in their fields from sunrise to sunset every day except Sundays. It was back breaking work and summers in Harris Neck were oppressive.

Georgia was the first colony to produce commercial cotton. The first planting was near Savannah in 1734. By 1860, cotton was the most valuable crop of the South and comprised 59 percent of the total exports from the United States. Great Britain consumed most of the output of the fiber in their textile mills.

In 1793, Eli Whitney built the first cotton gin on the Mulberry Grove plantation in Port Wentworth, Georgia. This machine revolutionized the cotton industry by mechanically removing the seeds from the cotton. Cotton production in Georgia increased from 1,000 bales in 1793 to 701,840 bales in 1860. With the rapid growth of this valuable commodity, the Port of Savannah became an international shipping center.

Cotton thrived in the saline environment found on Georgia's coast and its barrier islands. Cotton planting took place in April. It is a highly labor intensive crop. Over the next four months, slaves cultivated the plants and weeded the cotton rows. In August, the plantation slaves harvested the crop. It was critical to gather the cotton as soon as the pods began to break. It would normally require 10 to 12 pickings to completely harvest the crop. Once the cotton was picked, it was dried in the sun, moved to barns, ginned with roller gins and handpicked for market.

The most difficult part of the process was picking the fragile raw cotton. For 13 hours a day, slaves, including small children, would carefully pull the white, fluffy lint from the boll. The objective was to do so without cutting your hands on the sharp end of the boll. If injured or bleeding, there wasn't a doctor or nurse on call. Those who toiled in the cotton fields suffered under intolerable conditions. To refuse to work, enslaved persons were severely whipped and often separated from their families. Many slave owners did not hesitate to sell their workers to other plantations.

Cotton was king. Southern planters supplied 75 percent of the world's cotton. The planters became wealthy, while those who actually produced the crop silently suffered from the intense heat and the lack of hope that their lives would improve in the future. According to Yale University's Sterling Professor, David W. Blight, the financial value of all slaves in the south in 1860 was $3.5 billion dollars. This would have represented the largest single financial asset in the entire U.S. economy.

William Thomas Harris, Jr., married Margret Ann Harper of Lancaster County, South Carolina in 1785. Her parents Benjamin Harper, Sr. (1737-1801) and Martha Mary Knox Harper (1742-1815) were born in Belfast, Ireland. William and Margret Harris had three children including John Harris (1790-1847), Jane Elizabeth Harris (1801-1864) and Bright Baker Harris (1808-1875). When her husband William died in 1825, Margret married his younger brother, Captain John Harris, a veteran of the War of 1812.

Her daughter, Jane married Reverend Charles Joseph Washington

Thorpe (1792-1874) in 1815 at the Midway Congregational Church. She was 14-years-old; he was nearly nine years older than his bride. They had nine children including Charles Courtney Thorpe, Sr. (1816-1901). They lived on the Rice Hope Plantation in Townsend, Georgia.

With the death of Captain John in 1827, Margret Harris was legally willed the many components of the Harris Estate. Since women had limited property rights in Georgia before the Civil War, she co-administered the land with William John King (1790-1861). In 1853, she purchased the 1,200-acre Belvedere Plantation in Townsend, Georgia for $2,000. Margret Harris was living an idyllic life in Harris Neck. In 1860, she oversaw the 19th largest plantation in the State of Georgia. There were 482 plantations of 1,000 acres or more throughout the state at that time.

Based on the 1860 U.S. Federal Census Slave Schedule for Georgia Militia District 22, Margret Harris had 66 slaves. There were 37 men including Robert Delegall and 29 women. The oldest enslaved person was a 65-year-old man. There were 28 children under the age of 10-years-old. That same year the population of McIntosh County, Georgia was 5,492 persons. Of that total, 4,063 or 72 percent were slaves and 1,429 or 38 percent were white. Margret Harris was a queen in her kingdom in the Antebellum South. Her slaves labored in cotton, rice and indigo fields.

At the same time, William John King had 67 slaves in 1860 laboring on his plantation in Spring Cove, Georgia, a short distance west of Harris Neck. Nearly 40 percent of his enslaved workforce was below the age of ten. King, who was married to Martha Carter Cooper (1795-1856) died on February 4, 1861 in Harris Neck. In 1936, Margret Harris' great grandson, Elisha McDonald "E.M" Thorpe acquired the hundreds of acres of plantation land.

There is apparently no comprehensive description on how slaves were treated on the Harris Neck plantation. However, we do know that most plantation slaves lived in a small one-room cabin with dirt floors and little, if any, furniture. In Harris Neck the cabins were probably Tabby, a mixture of sand, lime, oyster shells and water, as hard as concrete.

Those working in the fields toiled for 12 to 15 hours a day except on Sundays, Christmas, and the Fourth of July. Cruel overseers, who punished and whipped men, women and children, supervised their labors. They were given just enough food to keep them alive and perhaps one set of clothes each year. Since slaves were prohibited from learning how to read or write, many of them did not know their birthday or how old they were. Since we know that Margaret Harris' white overseers cheated her, as is stated in her Last Will and Testament, there is no reason to believe they treated her slaves with any dignity or respect.

In her book *Journal of a Residence on a Georgia Plantation in 1838-1839,* not published until 1863, Frances "Fanny" Kemble, whose husband, Pierce Butler, owned the Butler's Island Plantation, just south of Darien, also chronicled the scourge of slavery and the wretched conditions in which Butler's slaves lived. In one passage in the *Journal,* Kemble wrote, "On my return to our island (Butler's Island), I visited another of the hospitals, and the settlements in which it belonged. The condition of these places and their inhabitants is, of course, the same all over the plantation, and if I were to describe them I should but weary you with a repetition of identical phenomena: filthy, wretched, almost naked, always bare-legged and bare footed children; neglect, ignorant, wretched mothers, whose apparent indifference to the plight of their offspring, and utter incapacity to alter it, are the inevitable result of their slavery."

After watching slaves toil in the rice fields Fanny told her readers: "In the north we could not hope to keep the worst and poorest servant for a single day in the wretched discomfort in which Negro servants are forced habitually to live." As an eyewitness to the horrors of plantation life, this English actress could never justify the evil and depravation before the Civil War in Georgia.

On April 19, 1861, President Lincoln issued Proclamation 81. This document declared a blockade of seaports in rebellious southern states, thus directly affecting the livelihoods of plantation owners throughout Georgia, including Margret Harris. The scope of this decision was vast. It covered 3,500 miles of coastline and 180 ports. The job of enforcing the blockade was given to 500 Union ironclad ships. The purpose of the Proclamation was to authorize the Union navy to ensure that, "A competent force will be posted so as to prevent entrance and exit of vessels from the ports."

Among the affected ports in Georgia were Brunswick, Darien, St. Mary's and Savannah. On May 27, 1861, the international Port of Savannah was closed, and it would remain blockaded for the rest of the Civil War. The net effect was to kill the export of cotton and rice and to impede the smuggling of war materials into the Confederacy. As a result, the economy of McIntosh Country crumbled. The days of wine and roses for Georgia plantation owners were gone. Instead of planting cotton and rice, they had no choice but to plant subsistence crops to feed themselves and their slave labor force.

On June 11, 1863, Union forces arrived in Darien. This county seat is about 25 miles south of Harris Neck. On that fateful day, Darien was abandoned except for children, women and very old men. Despite having little strategic value and offering no military resistance, Union Colonel James Montgomery ordered his three war ships to land at the Darien pier.

Colonel Montgomery was a Kansas native. During the 1850's, our 34th state experienced a period known as Bloody Kansas. Montgomery was a Jayhawker. He was a militant confidant of John Brown who believed the only way to stop slavery was to kill those who profited from this barbaric system. American Civil War historian, Albert E. Castel described Colonel Montgomery as, "A sincere, if unscrupulous, anti-slavery zealot."

When he arrived in Darien, Montgomery had three armies under his command. These were the Second South Carolina, the Fifty-Fourth Massachusetts and the Third Rhode Island battery. The first two units were comprised of freed slaves. Since there were no enemy soldiers to kill, Montgomery decided to teach the citizens of Darien a terrible lesson.

After his troops looted the entire town, he ordered the total destruction of Darien. Upon hearing the order, Colonel Robert Gould Shaw, who was the commander of the famous Fifty-Fourth Massachusetts Regiment (portrayed in the movie, *Glory*), strongly objected. Shaw was told by his commanding officer that, "We are outlawed, and therefore not bound by the rules of regular warfare." Montgomery also threatened to court martial Colonel Shaw.

Montgomery's troops burned virtually every business, church, public building, the Darien Museum, the school and all private residences. They did their job without mercy. In a June 12, 1863 letter to his beloved wife, Anne Haggerty Shaw, Colonel Shaw wrote, "I did not want the responsibility of it, and he (Montgomery) was only too happy to take it all on his soldiers, so the pretty little place was burnt to the ground, and not a shed remains standing; Montgomery firing the last buildings with his own hand. You must bear in mind, that not a shot had been fired at us from this place." Shaw also noted that, "Darien was a dirty piece of business" and said the controversial destruction of Darien was "A Satanic Act."

The burning of Darien occurred just six months after Fanny Kemble's book was published. Despite being just a short distance from Darien, the Butler Island rice plantation was abandoned but not burned down during the Civil War.

While it is possible those living in Harris Neck were able to witness the massive amount of smoke generated from the Darien conflagration, they certainly heard about it from their neighbors. From that day forward, there wasn't a single Georgia plantation owner who went to bed each night, wondering if their property would suffer a similar fate from Union forces.

While James Montgomery died peacefully on his Kansas farm, Colonel Robert Gould Shaw and 281 of his 600

African American troops were killed, wounded or captured during their July 18, 1863 assault on Fort Wagner in South Carolina. Eyewitnesses testified that these black troops fought bravely, courageously and heroically. They died for freedom and their sacrifice must be honored.

One of the survivors of this horrific attack was Sgt. William Harvey Carney. Born into slavery in Norfolk, Virginia, William Carney became a national hero. On that day at Fort Wagner, he watched the flag bearer killed. Instead of retiring, he courageously stepped forward with a hail of bullets all around him. According to the U.S. War Department, "When the color sergeant was shot down, this soldier grasped the flag, led the way to the parapet and planted the colors therein. When the troops fell back, he brought the flag, under a fierce fire in which he was twice severely wounded." For his extraordinary bravery, Sgt. William Carney became the first African American soldier to receive this nation's highest military decoration, the Medal of Honor on May 23, 1900. This was 37 years after his heroic actions.

On the night of August 3, 1864, a sizable number of McIntosh County residents met at the Ebenezer Presbyterian Church in Townsend, Georgia. Colonel William B. Gaulden, who was the commander of the Georgia Reserve Military of McIntosh County, had summoned them there. Despite being too old for military service, these men were the sole protection against Union plundering perpetrated on county citizens by both privateers and members of Union blockade gunboats.

At ten o'clock on August 3rd, the church became surrounded by 50 to 100 troops including Union sailors and freed African Americans. A spy had told the Union forces of the meeting location. While a number of civilians escaped capture, 23 old men were not so fortunate. Those taken into Union custody included 40-year-old Samuel R.J. Thorpe (1825-1889), 46-year-old William Thorpe (1819-1882) and 71-year-old Captain Armand LeFils. All of these men, except Captain LeFils, were marched ten miles to a site near Darien, loaded onto Union ironclads and transported to prison camps in the north. During the Civil War,

215,000 Confederate troops were imprisoned in Union camps.

Since he had spent a few months in the Confederate Army in 1861, Private William Thorpe was imprisoned at the Union Rock Island Prison in Illinois. He was paroled on April 1, 1865. His brother, Samuel R. J. Thorpe was deemed a private citizen. He was sent to the Union prison camp at Fort Delaware and was exchanged for a Union prisoner on March 7, 1865. Sadly, their mother, Jane Elizabeth, was not there to welcome her children when they returned from prison or the war. She had died on January 16, 1864 at the Rice Hope Plantation in Townsend, Georgia. She was 62-years-old.

On November 25, 1864, more than 60,000 Union troops under the command of Major General William Tecumseh Sherman began the infamous "March to the Sea." Union Commander Lieutenant General Ulysses S. Grant told Sherman, "The Confederates must be demoralized and left without hope. Take all provisions, forage and stock wanted for use of your command. Such as cannot be consumed, destroy."

It was Sherman's intention to bring "total war" to Georgia and in his words, "Make old and young, rich and poor, feel the hard of war." The goal of this military campaign was to destroy the Confederacy capacity to make war. However, what he faced on the battlefield was not the main contingent of the Confederate Army. Those 30,000 troops under the command of General John B. Hood had marched north to join the Army of the Tennessee.

Over the course of 37 days, Sherman's army would march 285 miles from Atlanta to the coastal Georgia town of Savannah. During this period, Union troops operated under General Sherman's Special Field Order: No. 120. This directive told his troops they were permitted to forge and confiscate livestock but they were forbidden from home invasions.

During the fog of war, many of Sherman's troops ignored that admonition. As historian Ashley Webb writes in the *Art of Hiding Personal Effects: Part Two,*" "These soldiers weren't kind to property, and they looted, destroyed and killed unnecessarily. They would hang men up on a slack rope and poke them with bayonets to make them tell where their valuables were hid. No room was safe from pilfering soldiers. Forgers ransacked the outbuildings and even slave cabins." These soldiers became known as "Sherman's bummers."

These bummers terrorized the countryside. Private citizens were hung or shot and women were raped. All sources of food and forage were confiscated or destroyed. Those who survived were left hungry, homeless, penniless and demoralized. These incidents were seared into the memory of the surviving white Georgia residents. Their hatred of William Tecumseh Sherman was insatiable and it remained so well into the 20th Century.

When not burning the state, the two armies engaged in a number of military skirmishes. The two most significant battles during this campaign were at Griswoldville and Fort McAllister. Griswoldville was the first battle of Sherman's March to the Sea. It occurred on November 22, 1864 and was a huge Union victory. Sherman's forces suffered

13 killed and 79 wounded. The Confederate losses were estimated at 51 dead, 472 wounded and 600 captured troops. In addition, Sherman's army captured a train with 13 cars loaded with critically needed military supplies.

According to the eyewitness account of Union Lieutenant Colonel Charles Wright Willis of Canton, Illinois, "Old grey-haired and weakly looking men and little boys, not over 15 years old, lay dead or writhing in pain. I did pity those boys, they almost all who could talk, said the Rebel cavalry gathered them up and forced them in. I was never so affected at the sight of wounded and dead before." He went on to say in his diary, "I hope we will never have to shoot at such men again. They knew nothing at all about fighting, and I think their officers knew as little, or else, certainty knew nothing about our being there." Colonel Willis spent four years in President Lincoln's army.

The second battle of Fort McAllister took place on December 13, 1864. It was an intense 15-minute engagement. Despite its brevity, 71 of the 120

Confederate troops were casualties; 209 of the 4,000 Union soldiers who stormed the fort, were killed or injured. A week later, General Sherman presented the City of Savannah, which he decided not to burn, to President Abraham Lincoln. In response the 16th President wrote, "Many, many, thanks for your Christmas gift."

In the *Personal Memoirs of U.S. Grant,* the former President wrote that, "General Sherman's movement from Chattanooga to Atlanta was prompt, skillful, and brilliant. The history of his flank movements and battles during that memorable campaign will ever be read with an interest unsurpassed by anything in history."

There is no question that Sherman's tactics, used during the March to the Sea were brutal, cruel, deadly and ruthless. Nevertheless, there is no denying that it undermined the ability of the south to win the war. The final tally was 2,300 Confederate and 1,300 Union causalities. According to Civil War writer, Myles Hudson, "Some 25,000 enslaved black people were freed on the march, including more than 7,000 in and around

Savannah." There were also hundreds of plantations looted. Some were even burned to the ground including the famous Mulberry Grove Plantation near Savannah, which had been the site of Eli Whitney's famous cotton gin invention.

Revolutionary War hero General Nathaniel Green established this plantation in 1736. One hundred and twenty years later, Zachariah Meshach Winkler purchased the property. Winkler paid $14,000 for 586 acres on a bluff that is now Port Wentworth, Georgia. Together with his plantation on Isla Island, he became one of the largest rice planters on the Georgia side of the Savannah River. In December of 1864, Winkler watched Union troops burn his main house and several outbuildings to the ground.

In addition, the vital rail system, needed to transport troops and supplies, was obliterated. During the campaign, Sherman's troops were instructed to heat the rails until they were malleable and then twist them like pretzels or neckties around trees. These were called "Sherman's Neckties." Unfortunately, for the south, there was only one manufacturing facility in Georgia to replace these critical rails. The economy of Georgia was destroyed and the Confederacy suffered over $100 million in losses.

McIntosh County was spared the wrath of General Sherman's army. Nevertheless, with the fall of Savannah, the war in Georgia was over. Military and naval forces of the Army of the Potomac had devastated McIntosh County but only Darien had been burned. Few counties in Georgia suffered as much as McIntosh. The loss of slaves and plantations was enormous. The good news, however, was that after more than a century, the nightmare of enslaved labor, forced family separations and barbaric slave auctions were relegated to the dustbin of history. Slavery was dead in Georgia and it soon would be terminated in the rest of the Confederate States of America. In the words of Abraham Lincoln, "Those who deny freedom to others deserve it not for themselves."

It was a glorious time for those now free men, women and children living in

Harris Neck, Georgia. Their prayers had finally been answered. Their suffering had stopped. They would decide their future. In the words of former slave Frederick Douglass, "What we now want is a country --- a free country --- a country not saddened by the footprints of a single slave --- and nowhere cursed by the presence of a single slaveholder." There was a sense of hope and optimism on that historic Sunday in McIntosh County in 1864. It was Christmas Day!

Chapter 2: Chains of Enslavement

Since the dawn of time, conquering armies have enslaved their defeated enemies. The earliest recorded manifestation of this barbaric practice occurred in 6800 BC in what was known as Mesopotamia. Assyrians and Babylonians who brutalized their neighbors dominated this region in southwest Asia.

In 120 AD, the population of Rome was about one million people. Half of those living in the capitol city were slaves captured during Roman military campaigns. Between 260 AD and 425 AD, the Roman Empire had a slave population of about 5 million people. This represented nearly 20 percent of the total population of the 50 million inhabitants within the Roman Empire.

In 1619, *The White Lion,* landed in the British colony of Point Comfort, Virginia. It was the first slave ship to arrive in North America. Onboard this vessel were 20 enslaved Africans who had been seized from a Portuguese slave ship by Dutch privateer Captain John Colyn

Jope. The landing of this ship marked the beginning of one of the most horrific chapters in American history. For the next 246 years, the British-American colonists and U.S. states allowed this abhorrent practice of denying life, liberty and happiness to millions of people to legally exist.

Like other enslaved people, those misfortunate enough to arrive in America were the victims of tribal wars. As the spoils of war, victorious armies sold their enslaved captives to evil, greedy and godless slave traders. This terrible symbiotic relationship was directly responsible for destroying the culture, families and lives of 12.7 million innocent Africans who were shipped to the Americas. Of this staggering number of people, only about 800,000 African captives were sent directly to North America.

In 1735, British Governor and founder of Savannah, James Edward Oglethorpe, banned slavery in the Province of Georgia. In fact, four years later, the Province issued the earliest anti-slavery petition in North America. Known as The New Inverness Petition, it stated, "It is shocking to human nature that any race of mankind, and their posterity should be sentenced to perpetual slavery." Oglethorpe's vision was to establish a colony with the utopian goals of no rum, no slaves and no large landed estates.

Sadly, the Governor's ideals could not withstand the pressures of competing with the slave holding states in the northern colonies. As a result, the Royal British Decree legalized slavery in Georgia on January 1, 1751. A key proponent of instituting this detestable system was the Reverend George Whitefield who was one of the original founders of Methodism. While preaching love and forgiveness, George Whitefield was a Georgia plantation owner who used slaves to finance his orphanages. Upon his death in 1770, Reverend Whitefield owned 50 slaves.

As an historian, I have read a great deal about the American Revolution. Yet, while in school, I had never heard the remarkable story of Crispus Attucks. There was a discussion in my college

American history class about the Boston Massacre on March 5, 1770 but there was no mention of the death of our nation's first patriot in our fight for freedom.

Crispus Attucks was the son of an enslaved African man and a Native American woman. When Attucks was 27, he escaped slavery and became gainfully employed as a merchant sailor, dockworker and rope maker. On that fateful cold March night, Attucks led a group of 50 colonists, upset over excessive and unfair taxes the British forced them to pay. After exchanging unpleasantries, British troops fired on the assembled colonists on Boston's King Street. Five colonists were killed. Crispus Attucks was the first to die.

In 1964, Dr. Martin Luther King, Jr. wrote that black school children, "Know that the first American to shed blood in the Revolution that freed his country from British oppression was a black seaman named Crispus Attucks. We must never forget the sacrifices of this Revolutionary War hero and the other 5,000 African Americans who risked everything to obtain freedom from the oppressive British Empire."

The first sentence of our Declaration of Independence declares, "We hold these truths to be self-evident, that all men are created equal." Sadly, this statement in 1776 was untrue. When this document was signed, slavery was permitted in all 13 original American colonies. Pennsylvania became the first state to outlaw this intolerable system in 1790. In 1807, the United States Congress enacted the Act Prohibiting the Importation of Slaves. It was signed into law on March 2, 1807 by President Thomas Jefferson and was implemented on January 1, 1808. By 1860, my birth state of New York and every other northern state, except Delaware, had prohibited slavery.

Prior to 1860, the United States Congress approved three compromises over enslavement. They were called the Missouri Compromise of 1820, the Compromise of 1850 and the Kansas-Nebraska Act of 1854. The original goal was to prohibit slavery from any non-southern state. Later bills, however, were desperate efforts to keep the union from imploding. The net effect was that six free states and four slave states were admitted to the union prior to the election of President Abraham Lincoln.

As someone who has long observed the actions of the U.S. Supreme Court, there is no question this august body has made a number of historic landmark decisions and at least one colossal mistake. During my lifetime, three of the most important rulings were Brown v Board of Education in 1954, Gideon v Wainwright in 1963 and Miranda v Arizona in 1966. Nearly one hundred years before I was born, the absolutely worst decision in the history of the U.S. Supreme Court was issued in the Dred Scott v Sandford case in 1857.

Dred Scott was born a slave in Southampton County, Virginia in 1799. He was the property of a farmer named Peter Blow. In 1830, he was sold to U.S. army surgeon Dr. John Emerson. During the course of his enlistment, Dr. Emerson moved to Fort Armstrong in Illinois and Fort Snelling in the Wisconsin Territory.

Both of these jurisdictions had outlawed slavery.

During Dred Scott's residence at Fort Snelling, he married 20-year-old Harriett Robinson. They became man and wife in a civil ceremony. This is critically important since slave marriages had no recognition in law. By having a legal civil ceremony, it proved that both Scott and his new bride were emancipated citizens. Together, they had a daughter, Eliza, who was born on the Mississippi River between the Free State of Illinois and the Free Territory of Iowa.

Nevertheless, on April 6, 1846, Dred and Harriet Scott petitioned the St. Louis Circuit Court for their freedom. They were allowed to file their request based on a Missouri statute that, "any person, black or white, held in wrongful enslavement can sue for freedom." Missouri had another law that stipulated, "Once free, always free." It said that slaves who lived in freed areas could not be returned to slavery. After much delay, the Circuit Court granted the Scotts their freedom just as it had to many other former slaves.

This was a remarkable decision by a compassionate and fair jury. Missouri was a slave state and would, in October 1861, secede from the Union. Sadly, the Scott's judicial victory was overturned by both the Missouri Supreme Court and a federal court in the state that unjustifiably ruled that Dred Scott and his family were still slaves.

In 1857, the U.S. Supreme Court had nine justices. The Chief Justice was Roger Brooke Taney of Maryland. The eight Associate Justices were John McLean of Ohio, James Moore Wayne of Georgia, John Catron of Tennessee, Peter Vivian Daniel of Virginia, Samuel Nelson of New York, Robert Cooper Grier of Pennsylvania, Benjamin Robbins Curtis of Massachusetts and John Archibald Campbell of Alabama. The court agreed to hear Dred Scott's appeal that he was entitled to freedom because he had been illegally held in bondage for an extended period of time in a free territory.

On March 6, 1857, the Supreme Court Chief Justice read the decision of the court. Roger Taney stunned the nation when he announced that on a 7 to 2 vote the court ruled against Dred Scott. The Chief Justice wrote, "It is the opinion of the court that the act of Congress (Missouri Compromise) which prohibited a citizen from holding and owning property is not warranted by the Constitution, and is therefore void; and that neither Dred Scott himself, nor any of his family, were made free by being carried into this territory; even if they had been carried there by the owner, with the intention of becoming a permanent resident." Associate Justices Wayne, Catron, Daniel, Nelson, Cooper and Campbell joined him in this racist decision.

The net effect of this vile ruling was that Dred Scott and his family were not entitled to their freedom and African Americans were not, and could never be, citizens of the United States. It is encouraging to note that after the decision, the Scotts were sold to Taylor Blow, the son of Peter Blow, who freed the family on May 26, 1857.

In his 67-page dissent of the decision, Associate Justice Benjamin Robbins Curtis concluded, "I am of the opinion that of the several acts of Congress that prohibited slavery and involuntary servitude were constitutional and valid laws." He went on to say, "The majority assertion that black people could not possess federal U.S. citizenship was historically and legally baseless." Associate Justice John McLean of Ohio joined him in contempt of this decision. In protest, Justice Curtis resigned from the U.S. Supreme Court.

The Dred Scott decision was horribly wrong and a major embarrassment to the U.S. Supreme Court. Chief Justice Charles Evans Hughes (1930-1941) noted that this decision was a "self-inflicted wound." It appears the vast majority of constitutional scholars believe Dred Scott was the worst decision ever rendered by the U.S. Supreme Court.

Five members of the court including Chief Justice Taney and Associates Justices Wayne, Catron, Daniel and Campbell were slave owners. They profited greatly from the labors of these unjustly held American citizens. They had a clear conflict of interest and they should have done the right thing by recusing themselves. Sadly, they did not.

A sixth Justice, Robert Cooper Grier of Pennsylvania was unduly pressured to vote with the Chief Justice by his good friend, the President of the United States, James Buchanan of Cove Gap, Pennsylvania. Grier also should have recused himself.

As for President Buchanan, he endorsed the legal basis of the Dred Scott decision in his inaugural address of March 4, 1857. This was two days before the decision was announced. Apparently, Buchanan thought this upcoming decision would help to keep the union intact. What is interesting is that James Buchanan, Roger Brooke Taney, Robert Cooper Grier and major slave owner Stephen Duncan all attended Dickinson College in Carlisle, Pennsylvania. This institution established in 1773 has the motto that, "Freedom is made through character and learning." For his inappropriate lobbying for this horrible decision and for his unwavering support of slavery, James Buchanan has earned the distinction of being the worst President in our nation's history.

The major impact of the Dred Scott decision was to provide momentum to the anti-slavery movement and it was a stepping-stone to the Civil War. It also bolstered the popularity of the Anti-Slavery Republican Party. Chief Justice Taney served another seven years on the court. He died on October 12, 1864. This was the same day his home state of Maryland passed a constitutional amendment abolishing slavery. Taney was 87-years-old.

Sadly, despite all of his tireless efforts, Dred Scott did not live to see the scourge of slavery forever banished from this nation. He died in St. Louis on November 7, 1859 of tuberculosis at the age of 59. There is today a monument depicting Dred and Harriett Scott at the Old Courthouse facing the St. Louis Gateway Arch.

According to the 1860 United States Census, there were 3,950,546 human beings held against their will in 12 southern states and the two Border States of Delaware and Maryland. The vast majority of slaves toiled on some 46,200 plantations. Products raised on these enslavement camps were corn, cotton, rice, sugarcane and tobacco. The largest slave state was the Commonwealth of Virginia, which had 490,865 enslaved people. This represented 31 percent of the State's total population.

The largest slave owner in 1860 was Joshua John Ward of Georgetown, South Carolina. He was known as "the King of the rice planters." Ward became a rich man because of the blood, sweat and tears of 1,130 enslaved people. He was active in the Democratic Party and was elected Lieutenant Governor of South Carolina in 1850.

The largest plantation in the United States was in White Castle, Louisiana. John Hampden Randolph built the Nottoway plantation in 1858. It was 6,200 acres of sugarcane fields. This crop was entirely dependent on the forced labors of 155 slaves.

While all slave owners were racist, historians have chosen Steven Duncan of Issaquwena, Mississippi as the worst slave owner. In 1860, Duncan owned 15 cotton and sugar plantations in Louisiana and Mississippi. He was worth at least $3.5 million. This represents about $125 million in purchasing power today. About half of Duncan's wealth was comprised of the financial value of 858 enslaved African Americans. Due to Duncan's cruel and harsh treatment, his plantation produced an extraordinary amount of cotton and sugar.

In 1860, there were 1,841 slave plantations in Georgia. The vast majority of those held in bonded servitude had arrived in the state by either South Carolina slave traders or South Carolina planters operating in Georgia. Prior to being enslaved, they lived in Gambia, Ivory Coast, Senegal and Sierra Leone.

Included within the list of the largest slave plantations in the United States was the Butler Island Plantation in Darien, Georgia. Major Pierce Mease Butler owned the 1,500 acres, where 505 enslaved people toiled for 70 years. The primary crop was rice. What was unusual about this plantation was that Pierce Butler's wife, Frances Ann "Fanny" Kimble was a committed abolitionist.

They had been married in Philadelphia in 1834.

Fanny Kimble was British. Her family were vaudevillians and she became a well-known actress, who loved to perform Shakespearean soliloquies. Unlike most women of her era, Fanny wasn't shy about expressing her political views in public. She hated slavery and the southern newspapers, which depicted blacks as inferior beings, who must be taken care of by their white Christian owners.

Fanny and Pierce Butler, lived in Philadelphia where he practiced law. He was also a big gambler, and his poor luck with this vice eventually brought him a great deal of debt. Fanny had often asked him where his wealth came from, and when she finally visited Darien, Georgia, she was horrified by the plantation and the extremely poor treatment of the slaves in her husband's care. She divorced her husband, moved back to England and wrote a *Journal of a Residence on a Georgia Plantation, 1838-1939.* In her own words, she said:

"The southern newspapers supply details of misery that it would be difficult for the imagination to exceed. Scorn, derision, insult, menace --- the handcuff, the lash --- the tearing away of children from parents, of husbands from wives --- the weary trudging in droves along the common highways, the labor of the body, the despair of mind, the sickness of heart --- these are the realities which belong to the system, and form the rule in the slaves experience. And the system exists here in this country of yours, which boasts itself the asylum of the oppressed, the home of freedom, the one place in the world when all men may find enfranchisement from all thralldoms of mind, soul or body the Land of Liberty."

Fanny Kimble was an incredibly brave woman who willingly gave up her husband, her children and the wealth created by his plantation. She would not be silenced in her efforts to speak out against the evils of slavery. Her journal was published in 1863. Pierce Butler's gambling debts and the money he lost in the financial panic of 1857 led him to auction off most of the slaves he owned in 1859. On March 2nd and 3rd at the Ten Broeck Race Course just outside Savannah, the Great Slave Auction, also called the Weeping Time, was held. During two very rainy days, Butler sold 436 men, women, children and infants. It was the largest sale of human beings in U.S. history.

On August 23, 1855, future American President Abraham Lincoln wrote about slavery to his lifelong Illinois friend, Joshua Speed. In his letter, Lincoln noted, "The slave breeders and slave traders, are a small, odious and detested class, and yet in politics, they dictate the course of all of you, and are completely your masters." The great abolitionist, civil rights leader and freedom fighter Frederick Douglass stated, "No man can put a chain about the ankle of his fellow man without at last finding the other end fastened about his own neck."

The Presidential campaign of 1860 was one of the most important in our nation's history. There were four major candidates seeking the office. Republican Abraham Lincoln, Democrat Stephen A. Douglass, Southern Democrat John C. Breckinridge of Kentucky and Constitutional Union nominee John Bell of Tennessee. The single most compelling issue was the future of slavery in the south and Western Territories.

This issue had reached a boiling point throughout the United States. It was a bizarre campaign. Stephen Douglass made stump speeches in numerous locations in the north and the south. John Breckinridge made one speech. John Bell said nothing and Abraham Lincoln stayed at his home in Springfield, Illinois. As the perceived front-runner, Lincoln was the object of hundreds of political cartoons that were blatantly racist. Abraham Lincoln was called a baboon, buffoon, fiend, filthy storyteller, liar, thief and usurper.

Despite not appearing on the ballot in ten slave states, Abraham Lincoln was elected President. He received 180 electoral votes and 1,865,908 votes. This represented forty percent of all ballots cast on Election Day. In the Commonwealth of Virginia, Lincoln got 1,887 votes. In the county of Fauquier, where I now live, he received only one vote from retired Union Major Henry Thomas Dixon.

Dixon was an impertinent man. Virginia historian John K. Gott wrote, "He disliked everybody and everybody disliked but feared him, because it didn't take anything for him to take a shot at you." After casting his ballot at the Upper Carter's Run Baptist Church, Henry Dixon rode his horse to the train depot in Marshall and boarded a train to Alexandria. He left behind his wife, his job and his fortune. Five years later, not surprisingly, he was killed in a dual at the Madison House Hotel in Alexandria. He had never gone home.

On March 4, 1861, Abraham Lincoln was sworn-in as our 16th President. He spoke to the nation and in particular to the seven southern states that had seceded from the union. In his inaugural address, he noted that, "In your hands, my dissatisfied fellow countrymen, and not in mine, is the momentous issue of civil war.

The Government will not assail you. You can have no conflict without being yourselves the aggressor. You have no oath registered in heaven to destroy the Government, while I shall have the most solemn one to 'Preserve, Protect and Defend it."

President Lincoln got his response on April 12 1861 when the newly established Confederate States of America bombarded and captured the U.S. military base at Fort Sumter. The President had lost his fight to preserve the union. However, the long overdue fight to end the barbaric inhumane system of system of slavery had finally commenced.

After the Union Army defeated Confederate forces at the Battle of Antietam in Maryland, President Lincoln decided to release his famous Emancipation Proclamation. This was one of the most important documents ever written by a President of the United States. The key provisions were that all slaves under the Confederacy were from then on "forever free." It also paved the way for African Americans to fight for their freedom. In fact, nearly 200,000

African American men, most former slaves fought for the Union in the Civil War.

These men were motivated to fight against their former slave owners for their families and the millions who had suffered under this reprehensible system. They were incredibly brave. They understood that in a battle with Confederate troops, they would be treated horribly and likely killed if they were captured. Each of these soldiers fought gallantly for life and liberty.

President Abraham Lincoln called the Emancipation Proclamation his crowning achievement. Nevertheless, it was not a permanent solution to ending this barbaric system. Sadly, the Proclamation only applied to states in rebellion. It exempted the slave holding states of Delaware, Kentucky, Maryland and Missouri. It was also entirely dependent on Union forces crushing the Confederacy.

Abraham Lincoln hated slavery. Nevertheless, he understood that if he immediately outlawed this evil system in the four Border States, there was a strong likelihood they would secede from the Union and join the Confederate States of America. This was something Lincoln could ill afford to happen.

Since 1804, the United States Congress has proposed, and the states have ratified 15, additional amendments to the U.S. Constitution. One of the most important was the 13th Amendment. The language of this landmark modification was clear. It says, "Neither slavery nor involuntary servitude shall exist within the United States, or any place subject to their jurisdiction."

While the Amendment should have been adopted easily, the battle to pass it was fierce. On April 8, 1864, the United States Senate approved the 13th Amendment, introduced by Senator John Henderson of Missouri, on a 38 to 6 vote. Those voting in opposition were six Democrats from four states. They were Senators Garrett Davis and Lazarus W. Powell of Kentucky; George R. Riddle and William Saulsbury of Delaware, Thomas A. Hendricks of Indiana and James A. McDougall of California.

After many months of intense personal lobbying by President Abraham Lincoln and more than a few backroom deals, the House of Representatives barely satisfied the two-thirds requirement to pass the amendment with a vote of 119 to 56. The final tally was all 86 Republicans, 16 Unionists and 14 Democrats voting Aye. The remaining 42 Democrats voted No.

The very last speaker on the amendment was the fiery Republican Chairman of the House Ways and Means Committee, Thaddeus Stevens of Gettysburg, Pennsylvania. In his memorable remarks Congressman Stevens told his colleagues,

> "When, fifteen years ago, I was honored with a seat in this body, it was dangerous to talk about this institution, a danger which gentlemen now here will never be able to appreciate, what "Some" of us, however, have experienced it. And yet sir, I didn't hesitate, in the midst of bowie knives and revolvers, and howling demons

upon the other side of the House to stand here and denounce this infamous institution in language which possibly now, on looking at it, I might deem intemperate, but which I then deemed necessary to rouse the public attention, and cast odium upon the worst institution upon earth, one which is a disgrace to man, and would be an annoyance to the internal spirits. We have suffered for slavery more than all the plagues of Egypt."

On February 1, 1865, President Abraham Lincoln signed the 13th Amendment. This step was not required by the Constitution since no Presidential approval is necessary to send the proposed amendment to the states. Nevertheless, the President wanted to send a clarion call to each of the state legislatures. Lincoln also referred to the Amendment as "A King's cure for all the evils." He was apparently referring to evening primrose oil, which was widely proscribed by Civil War doctors for a host of illnesses.

On December 6, 1865, Georgia became the 27th state to ratify the 13th Amendment. By so doing, this long overdue law became an inseparable component of the U. S. Constitution. The nation had finally embraced the philosophy of its 16th President that, "If slavery is not wrong, nothing is wrong." The last state to ratify the amendment was Mississippi on March 16, 1995.

President Lincoln demonstrated real leadership in getting this important amendment approved. However, there is no denying that his views on slavery evolved over the years. In 1860, Lincoln made it clear that if allowing slavery to exist in various southern and western states would preserve the union, he would support this Faustian bargain. While Lincoln never owned slaves, he was not an abolitionist who criticized the practice and even suggested that a solution was to "send them back to Africa." He thought slavery should be eliminated gradually.

During the Civil War, President Lincoln's views changed. Despite the advice of some of his advisers, he insisted that the Emancipation Proclamation be issued. This document was the repudiation of his previous ideas. Without Lincoln's untiring advocacy, the United States Congress would not have approved the 13th Amendment. I contend a key factor in Lincoln's transformation was his growing relationship with Frederick Douglass.

As one of the great freedom fighters, Frederick Douglass was angry the Emancipation Proclamation didn't free all slaves and that Lincoln wanted to move slowly to eliminate this injustice. Nevertheless, he recognized that Lincoln was willing to confront the evil of slavery and ensure freedom for all African Americans. This was something our first 15 Presidents had been unwilling to do.

The last time they met was at the White House on March 4, 1865. Frederick Douglass had just listened to President Lincoln's second inaugural address containing the passage, "If God wills that it continue (war) until all the wealth piled by the bondsman's two hundred and fifty years of unrequited toll shall be sunk and until every drop of blood drawn with the lash shall be paid by another drawn with the sword as was said three thousand years ago so still it must be said 'the judgments of the Lord are true and righteous altogether'".

Upon meeting after Lincoln's speech, Douglass told the President, "Mr. Lincoln, that was a sacred effort."

Chapter 3: Death of Slavery:

In his book, *The New Man: Twenty-Nine Years a Slave. Twenty-Nine Years a Free Man,"* that was published in 1895, former Virginia slave Henry Clay Bruce wrote, "This was the condition of the colored people at the close of the war. They were set free without a dollar, without a foot of land and without the wherewithal to get the next meal. Justice seems to demand one year's support, forty acres of land and a mule each." His brother was Blanche K. Bruce, who was elected in 1874 as a Republican United States Senator from the State of Mississippi.

Three weeks after Christmas 1864, Major General William T. Sherman issued Special Field Order 15. This order confiscated, as federal property, a strip of coastal lands extending thirty miles inland from the Atlantic Ocean, including all sea islands, from Charleston, South Carolina 245 miles south to Jacksonville, Florida. The order further directed that this enormous amount of land be redistributed to freed black families in forty-acre segments. This proposed policy was known as "forty acres and a mule" and President Abraham Lincoln enthusiastically endorsed it.

On April 9, 1865, Major General Robert E. Lee surrendered his Confederate forces to Lieutenant General Ulysses S. Grant at Appomattox Court House in Virginia. President Lincoln's reaction to the surrender news was one of jubilation. On April 11, 1865, he addressed a huge crowd that descended on the White House. In his remarks, the President told them, "We meet this evening, not in sorrow, but in gladness of heart. The surrender of the principal insurgent army, gives hope of a righteous and speedy peace." Lincoln's vision was to permanently destroy slavery and reconstruct the Union.

President Lincoln was a forgiving and compassionate man. There were no gallows or firing squads for Jefferson Davis or Robert E. Lee. During his Presidency, Lincoln issued 64 pardons for war-related crimes including conspiracy, treason and service in the Rebel army. Ironically, his first presidential pardon went to his sister-in-law Emilie

Todd Helm.

This pardon became necessary when the Union press discovered that Emilie was secretly staying at the White House with here half-sister Mary Todd Lincoln. This created a media firestorm in our nation's Capitol. The problem for Emilie was her marriage to Confederate Brigadier General Benjamin Hardin Helm who was killed by a Union sharpshooter during the Battle of Chickamauga on September 30, 1863. After receiving the pardon, she returned to her family home in Kentucky.

By winning this bloody conflict, Abraham Lincoln sent a loud and powerful message to the world. In the future, no human being would be sold like livestock. Husbands and wives would never be separated. And, no black children would be torn away from their parents and sold to some distant plantation owner. Slavery was an abomination, and finally it had been relegated in the United States to the dustbin of history.

Sadly, Lincoln would never get the chance to witness the end of the Civil War or implement his reconstruction plan. History was forever changed. For on Good Friday, April 14, 1865, while enjoying the play *Our American Cousin* at Ford's Theatre, our 16th President was assassinated by a fanatical pro-slavery Confederate sympathizer, John Wilkes Booth. Upon Lincoln's death, Secretary of War Edwin M. Stanton said, "Now he belongs to the ages."

Future President U. S. Grant was informed of his death at the Bloodgood Hotel in Philadelphia. He succinctly stated, "It was the darkest day of my life." When hearing the terrible news, Frederick Douglass opined that Lincoln was, "The best man, truest patriot, and wisest statesman of his time and country. Mr. Lincoln's name should never be spoken but with reverence, gratitude, and affection."

The death of President Lincoln was a monumental tragedy for all the citizens of this country but in particular for the four million African Americans who were now free from the scourge of slavery. In

one evil act of madness, their dreams of
economic independence and voting rights
were dashed. The nation would soon
learn that it was impossible to replace
President Lincoln. We had lost our
greatest President who sacrificed his life
to end slavery.

In an effort to appease loyal Border
States, President Lincoln had decided to
replace Vice President Hannibal Hamlin of
Maine with Andrew Johnson in the 1864
Presidential Election. As a former
Governor and United States Senator from
Tennessee, Johnson would serve as a
liaison between the Union and the soon to
be vanquished Confederate States.

Upon becoming President and after
serving only 41 days as Vice President,
Andrew Johnson pressured by the large
southern planters, revoked Field Order
15. One of his first acts as Chief Executive,
his order returned the 400,000 acres of
coastal property, set aside by the Field
Order, from Charleston to Jacksonville, to
the former plantation owners. These were
the same people who had declared war on
the United States over their desire to
retain slavery.

President Johnson strongly supported a quick restoration of privileges for the seceded states and his actions signaled the end of the federal protections the new freedmen had begun experiencing under Reconstruction. It was no coincidence that the Ku Klux Klan was established in Pulaski, Tennessee on December 24, 1865. President Johnson, who had been a slave owner, is quoted as saying, "The right to own slaves was enshrined in the Constitution." It was, therefore, not surprising that he twice vetoed the Civil Rights Act of 1866 that, "Declared all persons born in the United States to be citizens." Fortunately, the U.S. Congress overrode his second veto and the language become part of the 14th Amendment to our Constitution.

As a result of his policies and his utter contempt for the Republican leadership of both the House of Representatives and the U.S. Senate, President Johnson became the first Chief Executive to be impeached. The vote, on February 24, 1868, in the House of Representatives was 126 to 47. Every Republican voted to impeach but not a single Democrat. The U.S. Senate was one vote short of removing him from office.

While most of the freed African Americans in Georgia faced a difficult and uncertain future, those living on the plantations of Margret Ann Harris were given a different fate. On September 2, 1865, the "Will and Testament" of Margret Harris was signed on Saint Catherine's Island, Georgia. This island was a short distance from Harris Neck. In this historic document, which was never challenged, Mrs. Harris stated, "I Margret Ann Harris of my own free will do bequeath and convey to Robert Delegall formerly my slave ... and assign forever to have and to hold possess and convey all rights or titles vested in me to four several tracts of land lying and being in the county of McIntosh, State of Georgia."

This land grant was conditioned on Robert Delegall caring for Margret Harris and her then 57-year-old invalid son Bright Baker Harris until their passing. In the 1860 U.S. Census, Bright Baker is listed as "Idiotic." Interestingly, the "Will and Testament" also states that, "I Margret Ann Harris have tried white men and they have cheated me, abused and driven of my people. I now chose Robert who I have raised to take care of me and my son."

During the next ten years, Robert Delegall and his family fully satisfied the conditions of her will. By providing the necessary care, Robert gained legal title to these lands in Harris Neck in perpetuity. Over the course of his lifetime, Robert Delegall sold portions of the 2,687 acres of land to other African American families. These sales were to former slaves who had lived, worked and suffered on the Harris Neck plantations or to descendants of the freedmen.

Together these families established a thriving and successful community. They became some of this nation's earliest black landowners. In this stunningly beautiful collection of fresh water ponds, marshes, meadows and woodlands, they grew their own crops, fished the local creeks and rivers, hunted wild game and planted abundant fruit and nut trees. They only had to buy pepper and salt to flavor their traditional dishes and flour to make their delicious breads, cakes, cookies and pies. Everything else came from the waters and lands of Harris Neck.

Nevertheless, it was a hard life. No one in Harris Neck lived in a plantation house and even by 1940 the people did not have electricity, indoor plumbing, phones or paved roads. They worked tirelessly to provide security, food and opportunity for their families. While they were not wealthy in material terms, they were rich in land and "community" and they were economically free, a condition that the powerful whites in McIntosh County feared.

The vast majority of those residing in Harris Neck in 1865 were born there as descendants of those raised in the rice growing regions of West Africa. For generations, rice had been successfully cultivated in their villagers in Gambia, Ivory Coast, Senegal and Sierra Leone. Those taken by slavers in the 18th and 19th centuries were taken not in any haphazard fashion; they were taken for their farming skills. They were sold into slavery mostly in Georgia, Louisiana and South Carolina.

The people of Harris Neck were proud members of what would became known as the Gullah Geechee Culture, which has its own unique arts, crafts, food, language and music. According to the Gullah Geechee Cultural Heritage Commission, "It is the only distinctly African Creole language in the United States." Their language is a mix of African, European and Deep South words. In the low country of South Carolina and Georgia, these immigrants describe themselves as Gullah or Geechee, apparently according to how close to the ocean they live.

In Harris Neck, the Gullahs engaged in commercial fishing, crabbing, livestock management, lumbering, oyster canning, small farming and turpentine production. They had a wonderful life free from their former masters and local government interference.

Harris Neck residents made traditional sweet grass baskets. These very durable works of art required hundreds of hours of precise labor to produce the intricately exquisite designs. My wife and I purchased our sweet grass baskets during a trip to Charleston, South Carolina. We treasure them and hope to acquire more of them in the future.

As someone who loves outstanding food, the traditional Gullah Geechee dishes are some of the best in the world. The basis of their cuisine is rice, simmered vegetables and fresh chicken or seafood. Among those dishes served at homes of Harris Neck residents were shrimp and grits, fried corn cakes, crab or shrimp boil, Gullah rice, and sautéed okra and shrimp with a hearty serving of Hopping John. The key ingredient was always rice.

While the community was isolated from the rest of McIntosh County, they embraced capitalism by transporting their unneeded crops and harvested seafood to markets in Darien and Savannah, Georgia. They were never looking for a handout from the county, state or federal government. They simply wanted to live their lives and raise their children in Harris Neck, peacefully and without outside interference.

Prior to the Second World War, there were cemeteries, churches, crab and oyster factories, a general store, a funeral home, the Harris Neck School House, a Mosaic Lodge and a U.S. Post Office. While there were no hospitals in the community, there were well trained mid-wives, nurses and healers who understood the traditional medicinal uses of plants and herbs such as Cape aloe, Devil's Claw, Neem trees, lemon grass and turmeric. Only serious injuries required a trip to the hospital in Darien.

One of the largest employers in the community was the seafood industry. Many residents were engaged in the harvest, processing and sale of crab, fish, oysters and shrimp. Others were involved in the construction of fishing and shrimp boats and those essential items like baskets, buoys, crab pots, fishing rods, lures, nets and oyster tongs. The major local companies were L. P. Maggioni Oyster Cannery, Oemlers Oyster Company, Timmons Oyster Factory and Shellman Bluff Canning Company. Harris Neck watermen made their living plying the waters of the Barbour Island River,

Harris Neck Creek, Mud River, Newport River and Sapelo River.

In 1900, coastal Georgia led the nation in oyster harvesting with nearly 8 million pounds. Oysters are an excellent source of protein. Oyster shells were used extensively for the construction of buildings and roads. Unlike other oyster growing regions, Georgia oysters grew in clusters because of the overabundance of oyster larvae. The taste of these lovable bivalves has been described as briny, sort of nutty flavor with a hint of lemon grass.

The African American citizens of Harris Neck were deeply religious. In 1867, Reverend Andrew Neal established the First African Baptist Church of Harris Neck. It grew to more than 300 parishioners. Almost twenty years later, Reverend R. H. Thomas built the Friendship Baptist Church. Both churches are still active.

These churches were the heart of the community. Pastors were the Chief Executive Officers of Harris Neck. They provided not only spiritual guidance but served as mediators for land or property disputes, marriage counseling, petty grievances and unruly children. Pastors were always there at times of sickness and death.

These churches were the social centers of the overall community. It was here where a parishioner was baptized, married and laid to rest. Sunday picnics were lively events with delicious food, fellowship, folklore, stories and songs, which had been passed down over generations. They provided the fabric to hold the community together and to work together to build a better future for themselves and their children.

When the time came, there were two cemeteries ---- Gould and Thomas --- that offered a final resting place for their loved ones. Today, only Gould survives and is still being used. Many of its headstones date back to the early 1800's. Included among those buried in this hallow ground are Reverend Charles C. Dawley, Judge E. W. Lowe, Corporal Jack Thompson of the Union Colored Army and W. M. Thorpe.

In 1921, the Harris Neck Schoolhouse was replaced by a Rosenwald School. In the early 20th Century, more than 5,000 schools were built utilizing money from the Julius Rosenwald Fund School Building Program. Rosenwald made his fortune as a merchant who became the President and then Chairman of the Sears, Roebuck and Company headquarters in Chicago, Illinois. The idea of these schools was the result of the collaboration of Rosenwald and one of our nation's most prominent educators, Booker Taliaferro Washington. At the time of their first meeting, Washington was the President of the Tuskegee Institute in Alabama.

These two men were committed to improving the abysmal state of education facing black children primarily those living in the South. While the average donation for the construction of each school was $400 in 1930, they were apparently extremely popular throughout the south. The people of Harris Neck donated $1,000 of the $3,000 cost to build their three-room schoolhouse. Between 1915 and 1937, there were 259 Rosenwald schools built in Georgia. The last one was built in Warm Springs, Georgia and it received a $1,000 donation from President Franklin Delano Roosevelt.

Children educated at a Rosenwald school include poet laureate Maya Angelou, Georgia U.S. Congressman John Lewis and Civil Rights icon Medgar Evers who was murdered at his home in Jackson, Mississippi on June 12, 1963. His killer was finally tried and convicted of murder in 1994. As a result of the landmark Brown v Board of Education decision in 1954, the Rosenwald schools became obsolete, but those who attended them never forgot their importance.

In Harris Neck, there were distinctive communities including Carolina, Harper, Peru and Thomas Landing. The people of Harris Neck grew their own crops, educated their own children, treated those pregnant and sick, provided jobs and spiritual guidance to residents and buried their loved ones in their own community cemeteries. According to the Oxford Dictionary, self-reliance is "reliance on one's own powers and resources rather than those of others." Harris Neck was a model of self-reliance.

While there are millions of Americans who have Gullah Geeche heritage, among the most famous are football Hall of Fame running back Jim Brown, boxer Joe Frazier, basketball superstar Michael Jordan, comedian Chris Rock, singer Darius Rucker, Supreme Court Justice Clarence Thomas of Georgia, NASA Engineer Mary Jackson, former First Lady Michelle Obama and Republican U.S. Congressman Robert Smalls of South Carolina.

In order to honor the culture, Congressman James Clyburn of Columbia, South Carolina introduced the Gullah Geechee Cultural Heritage Act in 2006. The first purpose of this legislation was to "Recognize the important contributions made to American culture and history by African Americans known as the Gullah/Geechee." During debate on the bill, Representative Clyburn noted that, "One need only walk the streets of Charleston and see the art of basket weaving, the sweet grass baskets that are made there, and are coming out of this county." There was not a single objection to this legislation in the House of Representatives or U.S. Senate.

On October 12, 2006, President George W. Bush signed the Gullah Geechee Cultural Heritage Act into law. More than a decade later, the original author, James Clyburn, who is as of this writing the Majority Whip in the House of Representatives, told his colleagues, "As a former history teacher and historic preservation advocate, the establishment of the heritage corridor is one of my proudest achievements in Congress."

While it is important to celebrate the Gullah Geechee culture, one might ask: what was it like to live in Harris Neck before World War II? Here are the thoughts on some of those who lived this experience. In 1942, Evelyn McIntosh Greer was 15-years-old. Prior to her passing in 2018, she testified before Congress that, "We had a wonderful time as children. Much better than a lot of other black people in this country. There were five children in my family and it was our job to take care of the fields. Sweet potatoes grew here, and corn, all kinds of vegetables. My brother and I had the terrible job of tending to Robert Dawley's rice fields. It was almost impossible to discourage pesky rice birds from attacking the crop." Bobolinks loved to feast on uncooked rice in paddy fields.

Another community member was Kenneth R. Dunham, Sr., a talented carpenter. In 2010, he was quoted in a local newspaper saying, "Wildlife was a part of us all of our lives. In my back door, I could hear the wild geese coming. We left food in the field so they would have something to eat."

Harris Neck descendant and current Board Chair of the Harris Neck Land Trust, Winston Relaford, talks about his late mother, Anna Relaford, and her fond memories of growing up in Harris Neck. "One of the things she would say about how the community treated the land was, 'We always left some seed for the animals.'" Harris Neck residents believed firmly in the admonition of Teddy Roosevelt that a community, "Behaves well if it treats the natural resources as assets which it must turn over to the next generation increased and not impaired in value." Those living in Harris Neck were true wildlife conservationists.

Another resident was Henry Curry (1888-1989). Melissa Fay Greene, who described the political machinery and corruption in post-World War II McIntosh County in her brilliant work *Praying for Sheetrock,* described Henry Curry as a member of the first freeborn generation. At one point in his life, he was a sharecropper working on a farm. In her book, she noted that Henry, "Drowned himself in work. He whipped his hands through the cotton plants until his palms shone, harvesting potatoes or peas, until standing up at day's end dizzied him. As soon as he was able, he ran from that work. Not that farming itself demeaned the people, but the economics of the sharecropper arrangement was humiliating, keeping the people virtually bound to the land and to the land's owner." At 78-years-old, Curry became the first black member of the McIntosh County Board of Commissioners.

In 1940, the Georgia Writer's Project interviewed Harris Neck resident Eddie Thorpe who had been a slave. At the time, he was 83-years-old. He had been the caretaker for Elisha McDonald Thorpe's property. At the time of his interview, he was sitting in a chair on the front porch of his house highlighted by, "A small, neatly inscribed placard placed near the gate bore his name."

Eddie Thorpe's grandmother had been stolen from her home in Africa. In his own words, he lovingly noted that, "She come from Africa and her name was Patience Spaulding. She tells me that she used to eat wild things. I remember she use to go out in the woods around here and bring back some kind of weed she would cook. She called it 'lam quato.' It looked like pokeberry to me." This is a plant that must be cooked carefully because the berries, untreated leaves, roots and stems are poisonous. It apparently tastes like asparagus.

Another interview by the Writer's Project was with Isaac Baisden, a blind sixty-year-old basket maker. Isaac had learned his craft at a young age before he lost his sight and had been supporting himself making beautiful sweet grass baskets. He remembered the use of drums during his childhood in Harris Neck. In his words, "I used to dance to the drum. I recall when they beat the drum to call the people of Harris Neck to dance at a funeral. They used encouragement in having a setting up when someone die." Gullah Geechee burial customs start with a drumbeat to inform the community that someone had died. The funeral party takes the body to the cemetery but waits at the gate to ask permission from their ancestors to enter the sacred grounds. These funerals were solemn occasions.

Anna Lee Johnson, a 56-year-old dressmaker was also interviewed. She spoke about medical remedies, evil spirits and community gatherings. She recalled harvest festivals where, "That was always a big time. Everyone brings some of their first crops to the church and we prepare a big feast. We pray and give thanks for the crops and pray for next year. We eat and sing and dance. One of the dances was called the Buzzard Lope. We still dance it today." This is a popular southern dance from the 1890's. It was composed by Bessie Jones of the Georgia Sea Island singers and allegedly means, "A turkey buzzard getting ready to eat a dead cow or mule."

On September 24, 2021, Mary Dawley Moran celebrated her 100th birthday. She was born and raised in Harris Neck. Mary and her husband, Roosevelt Moran, Sr.; had 13 children including son Wilson Moran. For the past 80 years, Mary and Wilson, plus other outstanding citizens, have led the tireless fight for justice for the Harris Neck Community. While most people would have simply surrendered, they have never given up on their righteous struggle.

As the only child of Robert and Amelia Dawley, Mary Moran has talked about, "Living this great life in Harris Neck." Her father was a fisherman who built a shrimp boat he named *The Amelia* after his beloved wife. Mary had met her husband Roosevelt at the Rosenwald School. She had all of her children, except a stillborn, at her home with a skilled mid-wife and still remembers fondly playing "Hide-And-Seek" with her friends and singing "Little Sally Water," "When the Saints Come Marching In" and Baptist

Gospel songs like "Save My Soul From Burning in Hell."

Mary also shared a funny story during an interview with Dave Kelly in 2002. "Our school was right across the road from a creek that runs to Belvedere, and some of the boys would take their clothes off to go swimming before school. One day a friend and I took the boys clothes and hid them. The boys hadn't found their clothes by the time the school bell rang. I think they came to school rather late. One boy knew I had taken their clothes. I can't remember if Mr. Baisden punished us for hiding the boy's clothes or what, but he let us know, it was the wrong thing to do."

In the 1940's and 1950's, corporal punishment was an acceptable way to reprimand students particularly in schools in the south. Popular ways to address student misbehavior included rulers, paddles, straps and switches. My personal favorite was the 12-inch wood ruler with the metal side that was omnipresent in those years.

Although her son Wilson never got to live in the Harris Neck community, he once opined that, "We know that our blood of the blood of our ancestors is in the soil. This land (Harris Neck) is our land. We fought in every war to keep this land free, and one day, no doubt in my mind, we will go back and re-invigorate this area again."

In 1997, Mary Moran and members of her family visited their ancestral home in Senehun Ngola, Sierra Leone. Sabena Airlines sponsored the trip. Mrs. Moran was searching for her ancestor, a Mende woman who as a young girl was captured and sold into slavery. Mary was also interested in finding out about the origins of a song that had been passed down in this village from mothers to daughters for generations. The song had been found a few years earlier in a university archive in Indiana by anthropologist, Joseph Opola, who had been a Peace Corps volunteer in Sierra Leone in the 1970s. Lorenzo Dow Turner, the famous black academic and linguist, had stumbled upon the Harris Neck community in the early 1930s. He was told of a woman in the community, who sang a strange song in another language. That woman turned out to be Mary Moran's mother, Amelia Shaw Dawley. Turner recorded Mrs. Dawley singing the Mende song in Harris Neck in 1933.

Through a strange and perhaps miraculous series of meetings and events, Joe Opola following many diverse leads, first found the woman in Senehun Ngola who still sings this song in its original Mende and later found Mary Moran living one mile from Harris Neck. Mary's mother Amelia had taught her the song as a young girl, and Mary grew up singing the song not knowing its meaning. During the last several decades, Mary has taught the song to her daughters and granddaughters. The saga of the song and the connection it provided between a tiny village in Sierra Leone and the Moran's in coastal Georgia is beautiful and powerfully documented in *The Language You Cry In.*

It turned out that Amelia's song is an ancient funeral hymn. In Mende it is only five sentences, yet, its lyrics are beautiful, powerful and uplifting. The English translation is:

"Everyone come together, Let us
work hard; the grave is not
Yet finished; Let his heart be
perfectly at peace;
"Everyone come together; Let us
work hard; the grave is not
Yet finished; Let his heart be at
peace at once.
"Sudden death commands
everyone's attention,
Like a Firing Gun
Sudden death commands
everyone's attention
"Oh elders, oh heads of the family,
Sudden death commands
everyone's attention.
"Like a distant drum beat."

Harris Neck was a beautiful
community. Those who lived there prior
to World War II loved their lives, their
children and their culture. Life was not
easy in Harris Neck but as Mary Moran,
who spent her first 20 years there, said,
late in her life, "It was a hard life, but a
good life. Those days in Harris Neck were
my best days."

Chapter 4: War Comes to Harris Neck

On December 7, 1941, forces of the Japanese Imperial Navy bombed the U.S. territory of Hawaii. It was an unprovoked attack. In response, the United States Congress heard President Franklin Delano Roosevelt declare this dastardly assault as "A day that will live in infamy." Hours later, by a vote of 470 to 1, the U.S. Congress declared war on Japan.

Seven months later, uninvited and unwanted visitors attacked the residents of Harris Neck. The attackers were not the Japanese or German forces but representatives of the United States Department of War. While no one died in this conflict, the lives of those quietly and peacefully living in Harris Neck were forever changed. July 27, 1942 was their day of infamy.

Following the attack on Pearl Harbor, Germany declared war on the United States and sent five U-boat submarines to attack the East Coast of the United States. As a result of *Operation Drumbeat*, 6,000 Americans died and 300 ships were sunk during a six-month period. Two U.S. Liberty ships were also sunk off the coast of Brunswick, Georgia, about 40 miles south of Harris Neck. It was a frightening time, especially for those living in on our coastal regions. Citizens were instructed to turn off their lights, cover their windows and immediately report any suspicious ship movements. There was a sense of foreboding and helplessness in communities throughout the United States.

The U.S. War Department set about hastily building its coastal defenses and seeking additional sites for pilot training. In the southeastern United States, the Department was specifically looking for satellite fields for the Dale Mabry Army Airfield in Tallahassee, Florida. It was in Harris Neck that the United States Army Air Corps established a flying school in 1938. In early 1942, the War Department was engaged in secret talks with local governmental entities, including the all-white McIntosh County Board of Commissioners.

There were, at that time, thousands of undeveloped acres throughout

McIntosh County and several areas that would meet the needs of the War Department. One of the McIntosh Commissioners, Elisha McDonald "E. M." Thorpe, who had come to own more than 500 acres on Harris Neck, had also owned 3,595 acres of virtually undeveloped land next to Harris Neck. He sold this land to a Savannah real estate company only a few months before the U.S. entered the war. While Thorpe did not own a house or live in the Harris Neck community, he did own and operate a thriving oyster canning facility.

Despite several other viable options, on land that was uninhabited or virtually so, the U.S. Department of War was persuaded by local officials to choose the 2,687 acres of Harris Neck as a new pilot training site. The only land on Harris Neck not seized by the federal government was the 13.5 acres (Tract 140B) owned by Commissioner Thorpe. Instead of condemning this acreage along with all the rest in its taking, the War Department set aside Thorpe's valuable waterfront acreage, allowing him to continue profiting from his oyster canning facility .

This action also eliminated all of his competition within the community. Only Commissioner Thorpe was permitted to keep some of his property. He was able to do so because of his relationship with Georgia's First Congressional District Congressman Hugh Peterson.

The government destroyed the rest of the community - all of it except for Gould Cemetery and the grand house owned by rich, white Lilly Livingston, which the Army kept for its officer quarters. Livingston and Nellie Clapp were the sole white landowners, who actually lived on Harris Neck on a seasonal basis. (They were both deceased by 1942).

Who was E. M. Thorpe? Elisha McDonald Thorpe was born on July 19, 1878 to Charles Courtney Thorpe, Sr. and Harriett Elizabeth Thorpe on the Lebanon Plantation in Cherokee, Georgia. He served in the American Expeditionary Forces during World War I. During his life, E. M. Thorpe was a banker, farmer, forester, land speculator, seafood processing owner and turpentine producer. He also served as President of the Darien Bank. He moved into the King-Mueller House at Spring Cove Plantation in 1936. This property was on the western edge of Harris Neck.

He was also a public servant. Thorpe was appointed a U.S. Postmaster, elected to the Georgia State Senate and served for many years on the powerful McIntosh County Board of Commissioners. Like most of the 159 counties in Georgia, Commissioners are the Chief Executives of the county government. In other states, they are called freeholders, parish police jurors and supervisors. They approve budgets, enact and enforce local ordinances, hire county employees and oversee spending. In McIntosh County in the 1940's, there were five white men on the Commission, who were elected by all of the citizens of the county to serve for a period of four years.

E. M. Thorpe served as a commissioner until 1947, when he became the Director of the McIntosh County Coastal Highway Association. Thorpe had many important friends including the local Democratic

Congressmen Hugh Peterson and Prince Preston, Jr. According to Congressional testimony, Thorpe was no friend to the Harris Neck community. In one of history's tragic ironies, Thorpe was the great grandson of Margret Ann Harris who gave the land to establish the historic African American community in Harris Neck.

The black residents of Harris Neck were convinced that E. M. Thorpe was the main cause of their misery and pain. The matriarch of the community, Mary Dawley Moran stated in 2013, "We had a commissioner (Thorpe) who was against us and you know my daddy (Robert Dawley) said, 'I hope he is howling in hell.'" While Thorpe was only one vote, he represented the community and the rest of the northeastern section of the County (where Harris Neck is located) on the Board of Commissioners, and he made no apparent effort to suggest alternative sites to the Army. It is simply inconceivable that the War Department would have selected these lands without the approval of E. M. Thorpe. The people of Harris Neck contend that he and a few other county officials led federal officials directly to Harris Neck, right past the 3,595 acres Thorpe had recently sold.

Under the U.S. Constitution, a federal agency or department cannot simply seize private property. The Fifth Amendment stipulates that no person shall "be deprived of life, liberty, or property, without due process of law, nor shall private property be taken for public use, without just compensation." In the case of Harris Neck, the U.S. War Department could have negotiated with each black and white property owner.

Instead, it chose to condemn all the property, save Thorpe's 13.5 acres, via the policy of eminent domain. Under federal law, condemnation is warranted when: a landowner is unwilling to sell at any price; the acquiring federal agency and the landowner cannot agree on the value; there are defects in the record title and one or more landowners may be missing or unidentifiable. In the case of Harris Neck, all of these stipulations were ignored and treated as unenforceable guidelines by the federal government. There were several violations of eminent domain, including the black resident's inability to obtain legal representation and to get independent appraisals of their property.

Condemnation proceedings began on July 6, 1942 and the black residents were given just three weeks to leave their homes. The declaration of taking was signed on January 24, 1943 but the official day of condemnation, when everyone had to leave Harris Neck, was July 27, 1942. During their three weeks, residents worked tirelessly to disassemble their houses, barns and other outbuildings; pack and remove their lifelong treasures; and try to find a new place to live.

Those who did not work fast enough or who refused to move watched the Army and its civilian contractor bulldoze or burn their homes. Just before the July 27th deadline, federal officials and the contractor drove up to the First African Baptist Church to burn it down. Several residents stood their ground with clubs and axes, and one man said, "You burn this, you burn no more." The Army gave the people a few more days to remove their church, and working together, many members of the community took apart the church, board by board and moved it approximately one mile outside of the homeland to its present site. In 2022, the church celebrated its 135th anniversary.

According to various residents, the federal government promised to help them find new places to live. Nothing was ever done to help them. The government just wanted the people to get off their land, Evelyn Greer, a teenager at the time, told Mike Wallace in 1983, when he and his crew from CBS *60 Minutes* program visited Harris Neck, "They were concerned about us getting off the land. There was nothing about where are we going to live."

Whether or not the black landowners were paid for their land --- and there is no evidence in the thousands of pages of documents in the National Archives that they were paid --- what added great insult to heavy injury is the fact that everyone in the community was left homeless. Of course, this did not apply to the white owners, since none actually lived on Harris Neck. Families had to move in with relatives in the county or in

Savannah or elsewhere, while they waited to find land on which to build a house, find other cheap lodgings, or move far away. Harris Neck descendants are now scattered all across the country.

In the case of Evelyn Greer and her family, they found temporary shelter in E.M. Thorpe's barn. Amazingly, Thorpe charged her family, one full day's wages for every week they lived with his livestock.

Evelyn's mother, Verlancher McIntosh, was the long time cook and housekeeper for E.M. Thorpe and his family at the Spring Cove Plantation. Mrs. McIntosh was the only member of the Harris Neck community to have purchased one of Thomas Edison's musical Gramophones. In 1940, these beautiful machines could cost as much as $150, and this one provided Evelyn, her mom and many others from Harris Neck wonderful entertainment from the likes of Bessy Smith and Louis Armstrong. Sadly, it was stolen from her house during the mandatory evacuation of Harris Neck.

As for the Mary and Roosevelt Moran family of five, they lived in the piney woods, a mile from their homeland, where Roosevelt and Robert Dawley, smartly, first built a kitchen and eventually finished a house around it. Wilson Moran, the first baby born to a member of the community after the taking, was born in a lean-to shelter in the woods. He and his mother, Mary nearly died in childbirth.

To the issue of homelessness, the U.S. Supreme Court, in its 1934 decision *Olson vs. United States,* stated that those who have their land taken via eminent domain "must be left as well off after the taking as they were before." The Harris Neck residents also had their Fifth and Fourteenth Amendment rights violated with the Court saying, "appropriation of private property for a public use is forbidden unless a full and exact equivalent be returned to the owners." Additionally, the Court stated, "That equivalent is the market value of the property at the time of the taking, contemporaneously paid in money."

When asked why the community did not resist or refuse to leave their homes, though some, such as Robert Dawley, did refuse, there were three reasons given. First, the United States was at war. The people living in Harris Neck were patriotic Americans. Many of them had served in various branches of our military as far back as the Civil War and they wanted to fight against the Nazis and Japanese. Evelyn Greer provided the second reason: "They believed so deeply in their government. You could not tell them the (federal) government would lie."

The third reason was the promise made by representatives of the U.S. War Department that at the end of the war, Harris Neck would be returned to them. Among those who heard this promise, from two federal officials --- a Mr. Banks and a Colonel Chambers --- was James Campbell who, with his father, was told, "Don't move too far away. After the war, you'll get your land back." Wilson Moran vividly remembers his grandfather, Robert Dawley, telling him, "I'll never forget even the kind of car the man was driving, a brand-new Pontiac station wagon. A gray station-wagon."

Reverend Robert Thorpe, who was raised by Mr. Dawley, wrote an article on July 26, 2012 for the online edition of *The Savannah Morning News.* He informed the readers that, "The federal government condemned our homeland to build an airfield for fighter pilot training. There was a lot of other land close by that was all but uninhabited where that airfield could have been built, but they took ours. So, we did our patriotic duty and left. We were promised that we could return when the war was over. Now people say, 'There's no record of that promise.' Well, I was there."

Mary Dawley Moran said, "They told us not to move too far away because we would be the first ones to get our home back." Edgar Timmons, Jr., observed, "They promised my family they would give it back. I heard my grandfather (William Timmons) tell us many times that the government had promised we could return at the end of World War II." There were many others in the community who heard the same promise.

Reflecting on the promise, it is clear this was a cynical effort by representatives of the federal government to get the black property owners to peacefully surrender their land without incident. July 27, 1942 was a terrible day in American history. On that fateful, rainy Monday, government contractors entered Harris Neck and began to systematically destroy everything in the community that had not been moved. Houses and other buildings were bulldozed or burnt to the ground. All the crops that were not ready for harvesting were burned. Even Thomas Cemetery, the community's second burial ground, was destroyed. It was either paved over by runways or taxi strips, or the graves were dug up and dumped in a landfill. No one living knows for sure. Once again, the War Department broke a promise to the community.

Other than Gould Cemetery, the only survivor of the condemned lands was the Lilly Livingston House. This palatial mansion was built in 1889 on the site of the Peru Plantation by tobacco magnet and thoroughbred horse owner, Pierre J. Lorillard IV (1833-1901). The estate consisted of a two-story lodge, a deep-water dock, horse stables, indoor swimming pool and formal gardens with reflecting pools and fountains. Only the ruins of a wading pool and part of the foundation remain today.

Lorillard and his mistress, Lily Livingston lived in this mansion seasonally. Their neighbor on Thomas Landing on the South Newport River was Eleanor "Nellie" van Blunt Clapp (1862-1937). These were the only white residents in Harris Neck. By all reports they got along well with their black community members. Upon Lorillard's death, Miss Lily Livingston received legal title to the Lorillard property, and she lived there through the late 1930's. Miss Nellie Clapp was buried on her land with her beloved horses. Years later, family members exhumed her remains and buried her in a family plot. Miss Livingston was buried in Canada.

On July 15, 1942, the United States Army Air Forces started construction of the three-runway, triangle-style airfield. The mission of the 1,200-acre base was to train fighter pilots and perform coastal surveillance. Upon completion of the airfield, there were many prefabricated buildings used as administrative offices, barracks, boiler rooms, chapel, hospital, non-commissioned officers club, post exchange, pumping stations, recreational faculties, repair shops and a theater. The airbase was activated on January 28, 1943. At its peak in September 1944, there were 129 officers and 575 enlisted personnel assigned to the Harris Neck Army Airbase.

During the 671 days the base was operational, hundreds of rookie pilots were instructed how to safely fly B-13 Valiants, P-39 Aircobras and P-40 Kittyhawks. These were all single engine and fixed wing aircraft. The two known units assigned to the airfield were the 499th and 500th Fighter-Bomber Squadrons. After successfully completing their training, these American fighter pilots flew missions throughout Europe and the Pacific.

On November 30, 1944, the Harris Neck Army Airfield was deactivated. The U.S. Department of War assigned the airmen to different bases and some of its assets were removed. This date is critically important. When the base closed, not a single Harris Neck property owner had yet to receive any federal compensation for their condemned land. This was a serious violation of eminent domain.

This created a golden opportunity. The federal government could have honored its promise by immediately returning title to the rightful Harris Neck residents. These folks, black and white, had done their part to support the U.S. war effort by allowing the United States Army to use their property for free. Sadly, no such offer was ever made, and the former black residents of Harris Neck were left with the stunning reality that the promises made to them, just two years earlier, were nothing more than empty words. Their government had repeatedly lied to them.

In February of 1948, the United States District Court for the Southern District Court of Georgia issued its final rulings in the Harris Neck condemnation cases. This was nearly six years after the federal government had seized the property and more than three years since the Army Base was closed. At the time of condemnation, there were 84 landowners. Compensation was determined by jury verdicts in nine separate judgments. There was no compensation for businesses, homes, crops or improvements to each property including barns, fences, gardens, horse stables or other structures. Only the land itself would be compensated, based on the "fair market" value of each acre as determined by the U.S. government. This was a highly unusual procedure. Other federal agencies, like the U.S. Fish and Wildlife Service, had always paid for both land and improvements. And, as mentioned earlier, the black owners did not receive independent property appraisals.

There were 171 tracts of land within Harris Neck. The total amount paid by the court was $88,852 for 2,504 acres of land. Of this total, 59 black and six racial unidentified landowners, who had 105 tracts, were paid $30,343 for 1,021.5 acres. There were additional payments of $4,760 for the 4.92 acres previously owned by the First African Baptist

Church, Home Guild Lodge, McIntosh County Board of Education and Mosaic Lodge.

The 19 white property owners held 61 tracts totaling 1,477 acres. They were paid $53,749. The top three recipients were all absentee white landowners. This category included the Livingston estate of 328 acres ($28,974); E.M. Thorpe's 537 acres ($13,758); and Irvin Davis' 410 acres ($4,349).

The top three African American plaintiffs were William Timmons, who owned 322 acres ($4,002), the estate of Eddie Thorpe, who had owned 114 acres in Harris Neck ($3,914) and the 100-acre estate of Dan Mifflin ($2,470). The most glaring realization in these figures is the fact that William Timmons received $24,900 less than the estate of Lily Livingston, despite owning just four fewer acres. In fact, the Livingston Estate received $88 per acre, while the Timmons property got a mere $12 per acre. How can there be such a discrepancy? All these figures can be found in the 1945 U.S. War Department's "Final Project Ownership Map, Harris Neck Army Air Base."

There is no evidence the court ever explained the rationale for why the top two white landowners received more compensation than all of the African American and racially unidentified property owners combined. What the Southern District Court of Georgia did do, however, was to stipulate that these plaintiffs would not receive their compensation directly from the federal government but from former McIntosh County Commissioner E. M. Thorpe. How could this possibly happen - this the same man who helped facilitate the original condemnation in 1942, who got to keep his 13.5-acre oyster facility and who received the second largest payout of the landowners? There is no way of knowing if Thorpe actually paid the black owners. This compensation procedure was highly irregular.

There is also evidence that not every landowner in Harris Neck was paid for the property condemned by the federal government. According to the War Department's own documents, there are 349 acres in the community, covering at least three tracts that never received a dime of compensation. Also, a handful of

African American landowners still had their original deeds after 1949. One of those uncompensated property owners was Leonard Jackson Clark.

In a letter to Savannah Attorney Clarence Martin, Leonard Clark wrote, "I brought 80 acres of land at Harris Neck in 1934. In 1936, I built a cabin there. In 1942, Captain Cabell and his goon squad dragged me all the way from Harris Neck to Coastal Highway 17 and I got no pay for my property." Despite having the 9th largest tract in the community, Leonard Clark's name doesn't appear anywhere in the War Department's Acquisition Data document. By comparison, the estate of Nellie Clapp received $3,600 in federal compensation for 86 acres of land within Harris Neck.

In 1985, the U.S. General Accounting Office released a report on the Harris Neck taking in which it compared the price-per-acre averages of the land paid to whites, versus that paid to the black residents. The numbers are clear, and they show that the white owners were paid 40 percent more than the black owners. And, as stated earlier, the black owners were not paid for their houses or the numerous improvements they made to their land. Everyone was paid only for their land. So, if one thinks about the fact that all the white landowners, except Lilly Livingston, had made no improvements to their land, the disparity between what was paid to white and black property owners was much greater than 40 percent, had the government also paid for improvements.

Other mistakes in the condemnation process were that the compensation payments were allocated long after the 30 days stipulated in the court settlements, there were no public hearings on the condemnation of Harris Neck and property owners were not advised they could obtain an independent appraisal of their property. According to attorney Dan Biersdorf, one of our nation's most prominent eminent domain attorneys, "There were many violations of due process and people's civil rights in this implementation of eminent domain in 1942. The official eviction date in Harris Neck was July 27, 1942. Since this taking was wrong and illegal, all subsequent transfers of title, including the last transfer to the U.S. Department of the Interior, should be considered invalid."

On November 15, 1945, Major General James A. Ulio, the Adjutant General to the Secretary of the U.S. Department of War, Robert P. Patterson declared Harris Neck Army Airfield as surplus property. The federal government was now given a second chance to fulfill the promise made to the former Harris Neck residents. Sadly, once again, they were not afforded the opportunity to return home and rebuild their businesses, churches, homes, school and their lives. It was a bitter pill to swallow.

Initially, former McIntosh County Commissioner E.M. Thorpe wanted the entire property conveyed to the Morgan's Chapel United Methodist Church in Townsend, Georgia. He expressed those views in a letter to Senator Richard Russell dated October 1, 1946. Two years later, he had changed his mind. This time he wrote to Georgia's other U. S. Senator Walter F. George. In his correspondence, E. M. Thorpe noted that, "I phoned you from Atlanta about two weeks ago about the church getting about 145 acres in the air base here. Please do your utmost to get a full release right away and let the M.C. Church have it without any strings tied to it." He signed the note, "I am sincerely, your friend." None of this land was ever given to the Methodist Church.

Instead of returning the land to the people, the federal government utilized authority granted to them by Section 13 of the Surplus Property Act of 1944 (P. L. 78-487). Under this law, federal, state and local governments are given the right of first refusal - before the former property owners - of the surplus property. On April 30, 1948, the War Assets Administration informed the McIntosh County Board of Commissioners that they would receive title to "all land, buildings, utilities, and equipment comprising Harris Neck AAF."

The county obtained title to all of Harris Neck except for the 13.5 acres owned by E.M. Thorpe and the small Gould Cemetery. The only stipulation was that McIntosh County use the airfield lands as a county or municipal airport. The Board of Commissioners agreed. Upon receiving the lands, McIntosh County Attorney Paul J. Varner declared there were "Big Plans" for the maintenance of the air base facilities.

In another ironic twist of fate, the Surplus Property Act was repealed just four years later. Had it not been enacted, the people of Harris Neck would not have been fourth in line and perhaps they would have gotten their land back after the war.

Also, the Minutes of the County Commission after the war show clearly that commission members, at first, publicly discussed that they would attempt to get all of Harris Neck back from the federal government and that the county would then make use of the airstrips while the rest of the land would be returned to the former property owners. Then, in the Commission's meetings over the next several months, there is no further mention of the landowners. The deal had been made between the county and the feds.

During the County's ownership, the airstrips were never used commercially. There were several reasons: the fact that Harris Neck is an isolated community in the extreme northeastern part of the county, the soil was unstable, there were already two nearby commercial airports in Brunswick and Savannah and financing was never available for such a risky non-sustainable project.

The only aviation activity that may have occurred at Harris Neck was the training of airship pilots who were assigned to the Glynco Naval Air Station in Brunswick, Georgia. According to the December 23, 1954 edition of *The Brunswick News*, an agreement was reached between the U.S. Navy and the McIntosh County Board of Commissioners to utilize a portion of Harris Neck as a landing and takeoff site for airships. It is unclear how often or how long, or even if, airships used Harris Neck lands.

While Harris Neck was never used as a commercial airport, there were a number of nefarious activities that did occur within Harris Neck during the 13 years of county ownership. These included: drug smuggling, drag racing, cattle grazing and prostitution. The Livingston House was turned into a very profitable and high-class bordello.

Over the years, many citizens also complained about the condition of the property. One of those was former Commissioner E. M. Thorpe. In July of 1950, he wrote to Georgia U.S. Senator Richard B. Russell, Jr. In his letter, he noted, "Whoever controls the base now has let it go to pieces and don't keep anything in shape. In fact, they have taken down and sold the telephone line from Jones Station to Harris Neck, a distance of 10 to 12 miles, the line should have been left here to be used by the people. In fact, whoever has been and is in charge of our good base has just about ruined it." This is a truly remarkable letter. In 1950, McIntosh County had title to the property, and E. M. Thorpe knew who controlled Harris Neck.

He was correct, however, Harris Neck was being systematically abused. According to a July 14, 1949 article in the *McIntosh County News*, thieves removed all equipment and fixtures from the abandoned airbase including: the boiler room, military buildings, pumping stations and theatre. There were arrest warrants issued, but no one was ever convicted of a crime. In 1958, when it was becoming clear that ownership of Harris Neck would soon revert to the federal government, McIntosh County filed suit against Sheriff Tom Poppell for the looting of the former Livingston Mansion. The total value of the removed items was about $18,000. It is unclear how this matter was finally adjudicated, but no one went to jail.

More recently on, February 27, 2011, Rocky Smith, who is a blogger and wildlife photographer, wrote in his "Mr. Write's Page" that, "After the war, the airfield was no longer needed. It was decommissioned and turned over to McIntosh County for use as an airport. Which was truly a mistake. For several years, while the base set idle, corrupt local officials and free-lance thieves dismantled the buildings and stripped the property of everything of value." It is said, among locals, that chandeliers, tapestries, beautiful antique furniture pieces and many other valuable items from the Livingston house now adorn the homes of some of the county's elite.

This blogger is correct; it was a mistake. Harris Neck should have never been given to McIntosh County after the war. The land should have been returned to its rightful property owners. There were three distinct opportunities to do so, but the federal government missed all of them.

Dr. Martin Luther King, Jr., frequently said that, "Justice too long delayed is justice denied." The righteous fight for justice for Harris Neck was just beginning in 1948. The federal government made several promises to the people of Harris Neck. They kept none of them. It is long since time to correct this historic injustice.

Chapter 5: Poppell's Playground

After World War II, McIntosh was the poorest of all 159 counties in the State of Georgia. It had a population of 5,500 residents and it was equally divided between blacks and whites. It was an isolated rural community dependent on farming, forestry and seafood harvesting. It was also a destination stop for people traveling along the East Coast to Florida.

In 1947, the legendary Sheriff of McIntosh County, Adam Strain "AD" Poppell (1875-1950) resigned after 20 years in office. His handpicked successor was his son Thomas Hartnett Poppell. This was a temporary appointment. The following year, Sheriff Tom Poppell won his first election by defeating William J. Fisher.

Thomas Harnett Poppell was born on February 21, 1921. He was the first son of AD Poppell and Jane "Janie" Smith Poppell (1891-1979). On June 2, 1941, he enlisted in the United States Navy and served on the U.S.S- SC 1271. This ship was a submarine chaser, a wooden craft designed to detect mines. Tom Poppell was honorably discharged with the rank of Motor Machinists Mate 2nd Class. He married Nell De Loach (1923-2011) of Glennville, Tattnall County, Georgia. They had a son Thomas Harnett Poppell, Jr.

Although Tom Poppell was not highly educated, he was charismatic, cunning, ruthless and shrewd. During his 31-years as Sheriff, he, reportedly, had his hands in every legal and allegedly illegal business in McIntosh County. He was an intimidating figure despite being just five foot nine and a slender 150-pounds. He had a fondness for Izod shirts, bell-bottom pants, white loafers and rarely wore a uniform.

He was elected Sheriff eight times without serious opposition. Every ethnic group in the county supported him because he understood the basic rule of politics: If you do favors for your constituents they will reward you at the ballot box.

Before the construction of Interstate 95, large commercial trucks would somewhat frequently breakdown or involved in accidents on U.S. 17 in McIntosh County. When a serious accident occurred and the driver ended up in the hospital, Sheriff Poppell would get the word out to black and white county residents alike and they would descend on the mishap. People were then free to help themselves to whatever cargo the truck had been hauling.

Poppell was literally winning the votes of these poor people by giving them bags of frozen vegetables, melons and shoes. Truckers knew they could not win any fight with Sheriff Poppell, so they simply tried to get compensation from their insurance companies. The Dean of Emory University Law School, Woody Hunter was quoted as saying, "Tom Poppell was Billy the Kid. He was Robin Hood."

In 1951, during his first term in office, Sheriff Tom, as most called him, petitioned the McIntosh Board of Commissioners, seeking a lease for the Livingston Mansion. He wanted to use the house and an additional 102 acres of the estate lands to operate an exclusive men's club. On May 8, 1951, he obtained the lease at a cost of $10 per year. During the next six years, he owned a club that offered its patrons casino gambling, drag racing, illegal drugs, moonshine and prostitution. While his lease was revoked in December 1957, the Sheriff was never indicted for any criminal offense. For a total investment of $60 dollars, Tom Poppell became a wealthy man and reportedly had the "goods" on many important and powerful men, significantly increasing his power.

In her excellent book, *Praying for Sheetrock*, Melissa Fay Greene quoted a local McIntosh County resident, Sammie Pickney, who said, "We used to joke --- and I don't know if this is true or not --- we used to say he was the only Sheriff in America who owned four houses, one with an airfield, and all on twelve thousand dollars a year."

Tom Poppell had a vast empire. According to Mellissa Fay Greene, "McIntosh County was a mini-Las Vegas, a mini-Atlantic City, a southern Hong Kong or Bangkok where white men came looking for, and found, women, gambling, liquor, drugs, guns, sanctuary from the law, and boats available for smuggling."

The county was once described as a "movable feast of Yankees" who spent their money on legal activities like gift shops, motels and seafood restaurants. And then there were other travelers who got caught in the illegal web of clip joints, drug smuggling, gun running and prostitution. McIntosh County offered a cornucopia of these opportunities. It was not uncommon for a northern tourist to spend hundreds of dollars at one of the county's gas stations or roadside stands, many losing their vacation funds, in this pre-credit card era, and having to turn back for home.

While the original intent of many may have simply been to buy peaches, peanuts and pecan pies, the lure of easy money was intoxicating. They became victims of an unwinnable board game known as "razzle-dazzle" that produced only misery for those who played. During this period, the *Atlanta Journal* ran a huge front-page headline, "Thousands of Tourists Fleeced on U.S. 17 in McIntosh

County." At the center of all of this activity, was Sheriff Tom.

He was the last of the old time Southern Sheriffs; no one would confuse him with Sheriff Andy Taylor of Mayberry, North Carolina. Sheriff Tom did not have many friends in the federal or state law enforcement community. The consensus law enforcement view of him in the 1970's was that, "The only crime that existed in McIntosh County was Tom Poppell's."

According to former Brunswick, Georgia police detective, Doug Moss, "He (Sheriff Tom Poppell) ran McIntosh County with an iron fist. He was a benevolent dictator, but he was a racist. He kept his eye on the black community. If a black person got out of control in McIntosh County, he simply disappeared. He used to say they took a swim across the river wearing too much chain."

By contrast in the 1970's, the Sheriff's constituents were some of the poorest in the nation. They were also denied a meaningful role in the community. No African American

Commissioner, City Councilman, Mayor or Sheriff had ever been elected in McIntosh County. There were no black judges, grand jury members, storeowners, bank tellers, bookkeepers, clerks, librarians, mailmen, fire fighters or State Park employees. This was more than 100 years since slavery had been legally abolished in the United States.

While Sheriff Poppell got to enjoy his multiple estates, there were lots of black owned homes in the county that had no electricity, plumbing or telephones. They got to experience the stifling heat of a summer in Georgia where the average temperature is 90 degrees.

In the year of our bicentennial, Sheriff Tom Poppell celebrated his 28th year in office. There were also other members of his immediate family who were being paid by county taxpayers. His mother Janie Poppell was the County Jailor. His sister Maude Poppell Thagard was the County Clerk and his younger brother, Adam Strain Poppell, Jr., was the Clerk of the County Superior Court. The

Poppell's were the most powerful family in McIntosh County, Georgia.

On June 23, 1975, Sheriff Poppell wrote a letter on the stationary of the Office of Sheriff of McIntosh County to U.S. Senator Herman Talmadge of Georgia. In this missive, the Sheriff wrote, "At the time the government took the area there were somewhere between forty and fifty families of black people who owned the area. They were told that they could get their property back after the war. I think it is a damn shame this land (Harris Neck) can't be used for the people who once owned it."

In early 1979, Sheriff Thomas Poppell was an extremely sick man, dying with leukemia. In an effort to seek atonement, he visited the First African Baptist Church in Harris Neck. He apologized to the assembled congregation for failing to help the community get back their Harris Neck lands after the airbase was classified as surplus property. He even made a financial donated to the community's fight for justice.

The Sheriff's act of contrition was laudable. As Christians, we are taught to forgive those who ask for forgiveness. Sheriff Tom Poppell died on August 15, 1979 at the age of 58-years-old. It was the end of the longest running Sheriff's dynasty in the history of Georgia. He had been the judge, jury and monarch of McIntosh County. During the last months of Poppell's life, his wife Nell served as Interim Sheriff. She did not run for the office in 1980. Without this deadly illness, there is little doubt Tom Poppell would have been Sheriff of McIntosh County for many more years. One of the Harris Neck elders told Dave Kelly that, on his deathbed, Tom Poppell summoned some men from Harris Neck to his hospital bed, but by the time they arrived, he had died. Was he going to name the names of those involved in the county in the taking of Harris Neck in 1942?

After years of misuse, the U.S. government filed a notice on April 25, 1961 to revoke McIntosh County's title to Harris Neck and it reacquired all of the land. At that time, there were 1,716 acres classified as agricultural lands and 969 acres as airport property. It was apparent that no commercial airport would ever be operated on Harris Neck. For the third time, the federal government had an opportunity to return this once again surplus property to the original owners. Instead on May 25, 1962, the U.S. General Services Administration announced it had reclassified the 1,716 acres as airport property and after a transfer of title, all of Harris Neck was conveyed to the U.S. Department of Interior. Since 1962, the U.S. Fish and Wildlife Service (FWS), an agency within U. S. Department of Interior has used Harris Neck as a bird sanctuary. This decision was cruel, willful and wrong.

In a June 13, 1962 press release announcing the creation of the Harris Neck National Wildlife Refuge, FWS noted, "Because the refuge was established by transfer of federal lands, acquisition of the new area (2,686 acres) was at no cost to the Department of the Interior. An existing boat dock, improved roads, fences, some of the buildings, and other government facilities will be used in refuge management of the area." The Fish and Wildlife Service also made the ridiculous claim that Harris Neck was, "The only place on the Eastern Seaboard where the Canadian wild geese would land."

As a result, Harris Neck became part of the National Wildlife Refuge System. This system is the only collection of federal lands acquired and managed for the conservation of fish, plants, wildlife and their habitats. President Theodore Roosevelt established the first refuge in 1903 on Florida's 3-acre Pelican Island. The goal was to protect brown pelicans egrets and herons that were being slaughtered for the millinery industry.

At the time it was established in 1962, Harris Neck became the 196th national wildlife refuge in the United States. In the Fish and Wildlife Service press release, the public was advised that, "The new refuge is an important link in a chain of national wildlife refuges along the Atlantic coast. A closely associated group of relatively small refuges, including Harris Island, Blackbeard, and Savannah, will make this area the only sanctuary for Canada geese between the Santee refuge in South Carolina and the

St. Mark's refuge in Florida." FWS also announced that Harris Neck would be immediately closed to the public thus denying access to those watermen who had used the docks for generations.

As of this writing, there are 568 national wildlife refuges. They are located in every U.S. state and all territories except for the Northern Marinas. The National Wildlife Refuge System is comprised of more than 150 million acres. Of the 568 units, 512 were established by cooperative agreements, donations, land exchanges, transfers from other federal agencies or Presidential Executive Orders.

There are 56 refuges that were established by specific Acts of Congress. These can only be modified by additional legislative action. There are 63 refuges that contain wilderness-designated areas and 63 refuges that were created to protect endangered species. However, Harris Neck is unique in the entire refuge system. It is the only land formerly farmed by slaves and then owned by freedmen, and it is the only one that was established on former military land. It also represents only .000019 percent of the entire refuge system.

There are 10 national wildlife refuges in Georgia, including Banks Lake, Blackbeard Island, Bond Swamp, Eufaula, Harris Neck, Okefenokee, Piedmont, Savannah, Wassaw and Wolf Island. This represents 512,006 acres that do not appear on the Georgia state tax rolls. None of the ten Georgia refuges was established by Congressional action. There are no wilderness areas within the Harris Neck National Wildlife Refuge. Only an Act of Congress, a Presidential Executive Order or an approved agency land exchange can modify the size of a refuge or return land to former owners.

Since its creation in 1962, the Fish and Wildlife Service has acquired about 135 acres that have been incorporated within the Harris Neck National Wildlife Refuge. In each case, FWS either purchased the land or acquired easements from The Nature Conservancy (TNC). This national 501 (c) (3) organization has long been identified as a real estate agent for the federal government.

When private citizens are reluctant to sell their land directly to the federal government, they negotiate with The Nature Conservancy, which is happy to buy the land. Upon obtaining title, TNC sells or donates the property to federal agencies, like the FWS, for a very tidy profit. In the case of Harris Neck, there were two interesting transactions.

The first occurred in 1985 when FWS obtained an easement on 70.57 acres of land from TNC as part of a land exchange. The second acquisition occurred in 1981 when FWS purchased the fee title for 62 acres from TNC. The taxpayer cost was $450,000. The original owner was E.M. Thorpe's grandson, Arthur Lucas.

As someone who has worked on national wildlife refuge issues for over 40 years, I have had the pleasure of visiting over 50 units in various states and one U.S. territory. During the last decade, I have walked the grounds of the Harris Neck National Wildlife Refuge on three separate occasions. My last visit was in February 2020. There is nothing remarkable, unique or irreplaceable about this refuge. Its mission is identical to dozens of other refuge units in the region. Like most federal land agencies, the FWS is world-class in acquiring private property for inclusion in the refuge system. What is interesting is that the agency does not use eminent domain or forced condemnation to acquire private property.

FWS fails to properly maintain many of its refuges. The Harris Neck National Wildlife Refuge is no exception. During my last visit, the refuge was badly overgrown and desperately needed to have its growing forest floor fuel load controlled by proscribed burns. Without expedited action, the 663 acres of mixed Pine/Oak Forests are prime candidates for a massive fire. This would have a devastating impact on the federally listed wood storks that roost on refuge lands. Just a few years ago, the Brown Bark beetle was responsible for the loss of a great deal of woodlands in Harris Neck. FWS knew about the beetles presence the year before it was forced to cut hundreds of acres of trees but chose, for whatever reasons, not to act until it was much too late.

Prior to COVID, the FWS refuge website indicated that some 90,000 people visited this refuge each year. This number is highly inflated. During my three visits, I shared the refuge with a handful of people and there were only a few signatures on the refuge visitor logbook. It's also hard to imagine that more than ten adults could comfortably fit in the tiny FWS Visitor Contact Station. Dave Kelly has spent hundreds of hours walking Harris Neck, since he moved to McIntosh in 2001. He says the 90,000 figure is overestimated at least six-fold. Dave talks to everyone he meets on the land. He says the vast majority is not from McIntosh or even Georgia, and that not a single person has heard about the former community.

In 1979, the Director of the U.S. Fish and Wildlife Service, Lynn Greenwalt testified: "Harris Neck is usually visited by 9,000 persons annually." What is most likely is that FWS is now including those persons who visit Gould Cemetery and utilize the public boat dock on Barbour River in its figures, however, there is no car counter on the road to the cemetery or the river.

For the past three years, the Visitor Contact Station has been largely closed to the public because of the virus and a lack of funds to operate it. This means that those who visit cannot see the information posted inside the building or ask questions because there is usually no staff onsite.

The Fish and Wildlife Service needs to address the serious problem of an overgrown forest at Harris Neck. It needs to vastly improve its maintenance of this property. And, most importantly, FWS needs to stop ignoring the contributions of those African Americans who lived on these lands from the slavery era until 1942. There is clearly a need for new refuge exhibits, signs and an updated and accurate historical timeline in the Visitor Contact Station. The public needs to know that Harris Neck was once a thriving, self-sufficient community, owned by hard working freedmen and their proud descendants.

If the Fish and Wildlife Service is unwilling or unable to properly maintain the Harris Neck National Wildlife Refuge, then the agency should divest itself of some or all of these lands. To allow this property to be consumed by a raging catastrophic wildlife fire would be devastating, especially to the habitat of the "threatened wood stork." According to FWS Supervisory Biologist, Bill Wikoff, "During the breeding season there will be about 500 pairs of wood storks at a pond called Woody Pond. They nest in trees that are on small islands and on man-made nesting platforms in Woody Pond." There are also the hundreds of nesting egrets, herons and ibis.

Prior to the evening of February 20, 1983, the vast majority of Americans had never heard of Harris Neck, Georgia. On that night, one of America's greatest journalists, Mike Wallace, shared their riveting story with a worldwide audience on *60 Minutes*. This program is the most watched news magazine in television history.

In his opening statement, Mike Wallace told his audience, "Harris Neck is a stunning 3,000 acres on the Georgia coast. To the 75 families who used to live there, it is a promise given and then broken by the U.S. government." During the nearly 15-minute segment, Wallace interviewed members of the Harris Neck community, the publisher of the local *Darien News,* Charles M. Williamson, Jr., McIntosh County Commissioner Alton Davis, FWS Project Leader for the Savannah Coastal Refuges, John Davis and Secretary of the Interior James G. Watt.

Charles Williamson stated that, "I don't doubt that some kindly person working for the U.S. government would have put his arm around these people and to console them, to give them hope, that after the war's over, you'll get your land back, after the Germans and Japanese have been defeated, you can come back here."

Commissioner Alton Davis was the son of Irving Davis who had been an absentee owner of 410 acres in Harris Neck. He told Mike Wallace he agreed the federal government should return Harris Neck to its former owners. He was asked why he had retained his father's grazing rights on the refuge at a very low cost. His response was that grazing activity had occurred there for many years without a problem. However, this was not true,

Davis had allowed his cows to graze within Gould Cemetery. Those who had relatives interred in the cemetery, almost everyone from Harris Neck, were understandably furious. Film footage from *60 Minutes* clearly shows former community members cleaning up the mess and damage made by cattle, which included the destruction of headstones.

In true Mike Wallace fashion, he didn't pull any punches in his interrogation of FWS Savannah Project Leader John Potter Davis (1933-2013). Davis was responsible for Harris Neck and some 57,000 additional acres of federal refuge lands in Georgia. Wallace posed a hypothetical question, "What would happen if 40 families were given the opportunity to re-establish a good going community with a school, firehouse, some farm land and a couple of roads, some kids and happiness?" John Davis' response was, "It would displace a lot of wildlife. They would have to go somewhere else. The disturbance factor would be too great. Just the mere presence of people continuously with people type activities that would occur, the displacement of habitat would eventually see some species leave permanently."

It was a shameful ramble and Davis' explanation was absurd and quite hilarious. The truth is that people have lived on this property for hundreds of years and have done so in complete harmony with the ducks, herons, owls, raccoons, songbirds, white-tailed deer, wild turkeys and wood storks. Wilson Moran told Dave Kelly that he went to a lecture given by FWS years ago, where FWS claimed that they introduced the wood stork to Harris Neck in the late 1960's. Wilson told Dave, "The wood stork has always been here. My people lived with them and all the wildlife, and they did so sustainably. And when my people were here, there were many more deer and turkeys; the wildlife was much more plentiful."

Before concluding his interview with John Davis, Mike Wallace asked him, "If (Harris Neck) this were to disappear from the face of the earth, this 2,687 acres, the republic would not be subverted and the bird and deer population would not die from trauma.

Would they?" John Davis' pitiful response was, "Probably not in all reality." If the mere presence of people is such a problem, then why does FWS allow year-round biking, birding, fishing, hiking, hunting and wildlife watching on the Harris Neck National Wildlife Refuge? It occurs because human activity itself has little, if any, adverse effect on the vast majority of wildlife species. In fact, regarding the "threatened" wood stork, every study of them that I have read calls for only a 100-meter setback from development. Many people in McIntosh County have wood storks and herons in the trees close to their homes, and people all over the United States see eagle nests in their yards, on golf courses and even along noisy interstate highways.

During the *60 Minutes* show, Evelyn Greer gave Wallace a tour of Harris Neck. Sitting in a jeep on the levee constructed by FWS at one end of woody pond, she told him, "How can you forget, going to a school for seven years, had everything you wanted and then just look around in a twinkle of an eye there was nothing there. Not nothing. Your church, your home, your friends. Everything is gone." Wallace, narrating, responded, "They lost it all. Their homes, their crops, the docks, the tranquility, the beauty, the community."

During his research for this show, Mike Wallace checked with the Department of Defense to ascertain, "Who was promised what?" The Department's response was an unsatisfying, "There are no records on what transpired back in the 1940's." This is a remarkable but not surprising answer. For 80 years, the federal government has issued excuses and lies as to why they have refused to correct this glaring injustice.

Before departing the community, Mike Wallace met with some of the young leaders in the community including Kenneth Dunham, Chris McIntosh, Jr., Wilson Moran and Reverend Edgar Timmons, Jr. Reverend Timmons opined, "Our home is on the outside of a barbed wire fence. Locked away is our heritage." He also passionately addressed the issue of cattle grazing. "When cattle makes waste upon your dead folks resting place, how worse can it get? We put up a barbed wire fence (around the cemetery). Someone go and clipped the fence. Those cows make waste on our dead folks. Right on top of them."

The Fish and Wildlife Service should have been ashamed for allowing this activity to occur. It should never have been allowed. In the eyes of the agency, four-legged bovines had more rights than deceased African Americans. Years later, during a contentious exchange in a March 2010 meeting between the Southeast Regional Director of FWS, Cynthia Dohner, and her staff and several from Harris Neck, Evelyn Greer said, "So, you are saying that these birds have more rights than people." Dohner responded, very unconvincingly, that such was not the case. However, the actions of FWS and the agency's treatment of the Harris Neck people over the decades sadly show Evelyn Greer to be correct.

Wilson Moran suggested to Mike Wallace a solution might be for the federal government to give the former residents 800 to 1,000 acres through a long-term lease agreement. For example, since 1947, the State of Georgia has owned the 5,700 acres of Jekyll Island. There are a number of black and white families residing on Jekyll, who have obtained 99-year leases from the state. There is no good reason a similar arrangement could not be reached in Harris Neck; most especially since FWS does not need the Harris Neck refuge. The bottom line is that each of these four men, talking with Wallace, agreed that Harris Neck, "Is the promised land." They want to go home and will not stop fighting until that long-awaited day arrives.

Finally, Mike Wallace interviewed in his Washington Office, the 43rd Secretary of the Interior, James Gaius Watt of Lusk, Wyoming. In his capacity, the Secretary had jurisdiction over millions of acres of federal lands, administered by the Bureau of Indian Affairs, Bureau of Land Management, National Park Service and U.S. Fish and Wildlife Service.

James Watt had earned a Juris Doctor degree from the University of Wyoming in 1962. What he told Mike Wallace was, "The equities are with the community. The law is clear and I must pursue that and there is not much I can do unless Congress would address and bring an equitable solution. Hopefully Congress will address this issue."

When pressed as to how to solve this problem, Watt said, "I predict legislation will be introduced that would bring relief to these people and that this Administration (Reagan) would be ready to testify and not object or obstruct this issue in any way." Sadly, Secretary Watt never had the opportunity to testify in the People's House. There were no bills pending before them. Congressman Bo Ginn left the Congress in 1982 and his successor Lindsay Thomas introduced only five bills in the 103rd Congress, none of them dealing with Harris Neck. Ironically, two of his five proposals would have designated the Bo Ginn National Fish Hatchery and amend the boundaries of the Cumberland Island National Seashore.

On July 14, 1984, Georgia U.S. Senators Mack Mattingly (R), Sam Nunn (D) and Congressman Lindsay Thomas (D), who represented Georgia's 1st Congressional District, wrote to the United States General Accounting Office (GAO). The Budget and Accounting Act (P.L 67-13) established this office in

1921. One of the primary missions of the GAO is to "investigate allegations of illegal and improper activities" by the U.S. federal government.

In their letter, these members were seeking responses to certain key questions regarding the condemnation of Harris Neck in 1942. Specifically, they asked: whether the land acquisitions were made appropriately; if property owners were fairly compensated; was there evidence of racial discrimination; were verbal or written promises made; why were agricultural lands designated as airport lands; was the U.S. War Department legally able to transfer Harris Necks lands to McIntosh County and how did Harris Neck compare with Ft. Steward Military Base, about 25 miles from Harris Neck, in terms of the condemnation of private property?

On May 29, 1985, 308 days after the letter was sent, the Director of the GOA, J. Dexter Peach, responded. The GOA document is 16 pages long and includes three separate attachments. It is frankly one of the worst reports I have ever read from this office. The GAO failed to address two of the most important inquires of whether the property owners were "fairly compensated" and was their evidence of racial discrimination.

The GOA stated they were unable to answer those two questions because of a 1981 fire that destroyed the Land and Property Tax Assessment Records for Harris Neck from 1920 to 1979. This was long before the advent of computers but frankly, it is unbelievable that these records would only exist at one location. GAO also opined, "The final judgment files contained an opinion of the U.S. Attorney (Thomas Campbell Clark), stating that full disbursement of funds had been made and that the condemnation proceedings were conducted in a proper and regular manner." It is unclear how much analysis the Attorney General undertook in this case and interesting that GAO used the term "opinion" but not "legal opinion."

The GAO also advised members of Congress that, "Only if surplus land was not classified as suitable for airport purposes, and not disposed of to federal, state, or local governments, was the federal government required to notify the person from whom the land was acquired of its availability and offer it in a private sale." In the case of Harris Neck, the land was never suitable for an airport because of the very sandy soil. Soon after the Army completed the runways in 1943, they started to crack, especially when the heavier supply planes began landing. In 1948, the federal government could have either given the land back to its former private owners or offered it to them in a private sale.

On the question of Ft. Stewart, it is inappropriate to try to compare the two military bases. The Harris Neck Army Airfield was comprised of 2,687 acres in McIntosh County. It was operational for only a brief period of time. By contrast, the Ft. Stewart Military Reservation has 280,376 acres of marshland type terrain. It extends over five counties and has been an active U.S. base since 1941. Even GOA noted that, "We did not review the Hunter Army Airfield (Ft. Stewart) land acquisition procedures and compensation arrangements because of the unavailability of government records." There is certainly an ugly pattern of a lack of proper records keeping.

While the GOA report was a huge disappointment to those seeking the truth, it did contain one important analysis. There is an old rural expression that, "Even a blind pig can find an acorn once in a while." This analysis was the one nugget in the report. Unlike the U.S. War Department's report that divided the residents of Harris Neck into two racial categories, GAO more accurately characterized the 84 property owners as black, white and racially unidentified.

What they determined was that 8 property owners were racially unidentified. They received $2,743 for 14 tracts of land containing 53 acres. This represents a compensation rate of $52.08 per acre. White landowners were paid $57,153 for 66 tracts containing 1,532 acres of land. Their compensation rate was $37.31 per acre. Finally, black property owners obtained only $29,653 for 89 tracts of land representing 1,102 acres. Their payment rate was $26.90 per acre. In the final analysis, black landowners received $27,500 less than white property owners and $10.41 less per acre.

The General Accounting Office did confirm they were unable to evaluate the acquisition payments, why black landowners received the lowest per-acre compensation and whether there was racial discrimination in determining the payments. There isn't a single African American, who lived in Harris Neck before 1942 or is now living outside the refuge, who believes they were treated fairly and equitably by the federal government. The answers to the Congressional GAO letter are clear: the land acquisitions were not appropriate, African American property owners were not fairly compensated, verbal promises were made and broken and there was plenty of evidence that racial discrimination was at play in a big way.

After receiving copies of the GAO's wanting report, none of the three Georgia Congressional representatives introduced remedial legislation. The longest serving of these three members was Senator Sam Nunn of Macon, Georgia. He represented Georgia in the U.S. Senate for 24 years. During that time, he introduced 313 bills, but not a single one provided assistance to the former Harris Neck residents.

The second longest serving was Congressman Lindsay Thomas of Patterson, Georgia. He represented the people of the 1st Congressional District during his ten years in the House of Representatives. He proposed 23 bills but none dealt with Harris Neck.

Finally, Senator Mack Mattingly of Brunswick, Georgia represented the people of Georgia in the U.S. Senate for one six-year term from 1981 to 1987. He introduced 61 bills during his tenure but nothing dealing with Harris Neck. This is somewhat surprising in the light of the fact that he was willing to write to the U.S. Government Accounting Office.

It is likely all three of these representatives either watched or heard about the *60 Minutes* show on Harris Neck, and were then motivated to, at least, write to the GAO. As a Republican Senator, Mattingly had to be aware that Secretary of the Interior, James Watt, had articulated in the *60 Minutes* segment that the Reagan Administration would not oppose or obstruct any effort to provide an equitable solution for Harris Neck. Sadly, these representatives did not follow up on the GAO report as they could have, and the hopes and dreams of the Harris Neck community were once again ignored.

In the words of our 44th President, Barack Obama, "Hope is that thing inside us that insists, despite all the evidence to the contrary, that something better awaits us if we have the courage to reach for it and to work for it and to fight for it." The people of Harris Neck, Georgia have never lost faith and have never stopped fighting, but they have waited far too long for justice!

Sketch by Samuel Beetler, II of the Robert Dawley House

Robert Dawley portrait
Permission given by Wilson Moran

Harris Neck, Georgia

The road to Woody Pond, Harris Neck

Rev. Robert Thorpe,
First Chair of the Harris Neck Land Trust

Harris Neck fundraiser

168

Community meeting with FWS Regional Director
Cynthia Dohner – August 2013

Community meeting in the Old Fellowship Hall of the First
African Baptist Church

Harris Neck Symposium, Savannah State University
Olive Smith, Mary Moran, Kenneth Dunham, & Rev. Robert
Thorpe – February 5, 2014

Young members of the Harris Neck community

The Harris Neck Land Trust meeting with
Holland & Knight
Pictured: Winston Relaford, Robert Highsmith, Jennifer Modrich, Chester
Dunham, Rev. Edgar Timmons, & David M. Kelly

Leaders of the Harris Neck Land Trust
Pictured: David M. Kelly, Rev. Robert Thorpe, Wilson
Moran, Chester Dunham, William Collins, Olive Hillary,
Evelyn Greer, Winston Relaford, Sr.

Chapter 6: Seeking A Solution

In this country, aggrieved individuals and organizations can obtain justice through court decisions, federal laws and executive action. For six decades, the Harris Neck community utilized our courts, encouraged elected representatives to sponsor legislation on their behalf and sought a cooperative leasing agreement with the U.S. Fish and Wildlife Service (FWS).

Following the distribution of the final condemnation payments in 1948, there was a growing resentment among the former black Harris Neck residents that their government had mistreated them. Even the slickest government bureaucrat could never convince them that their land had been properly taken, that they deserved less compensation, that they were treated like the white or racially unidentified residents in the community or that the government promises made were nothing more than a sick joke.

Despite their anger, disappointment and frustration, it wasn't until 1979 that the first organized effort for justice by those from Harris Neck began. The leading advocate was a group known as the People Organized for Equal Rights (POER). On April 27, 1979, some 40 former community residents and first-generation descendants entered, without authorization or permission, the Harris Neck National Wildlife Refuge. Their goal was to stage a peaceful protest and assert their claim to the land.

They informed John Davis, FWS Project Leader of the Savannah National Wildlife Refuge Complex, of their intention to remain indefinitely and their demand of $50 million from the U.S. government. These reparations would be used to rebuild businesses, churches, schools and private residences lost during the federal takeover. The government had never paid a cent in compensation for destroying these buildings.

During the next three days, a small tent city was erected, cooking fires were built and materials such as bags of mortar, concrete blocks and lumber arrived to build the foundations of their previous homes. There were also about forty automobiles and motorcycles used by the protestors. One of the visitors to the camp was 77-year-old Reverend Alfred Curry. Rev. Curry had lived in Harris Neck and watched in horror as his government destroyed his community in 1942. In his words, "It is a tragedy and to my knowledge the most pathetic act in humankind."

Instead of entering into meaningful negotiations, the U.S. government immediately filed a complaint for ejectment. The protestors were given until 5:00 P.M. on May 1, 1979 to remove themselves and all of their personal belongings from the wildlife refuge. On May 2, 1979, armed U.S. Marshals arrived at the campsite. They forcibly arrested three of the key leaders of the People Organized for Equal Rights. Those dragged away into custody were Hercules Anderson, Chris McIntosh, Jr. and Reverend Edgar Timmons, Jr. The marshals also arrested Reverend Ted Clark, who was the Economic Development Director of the Southern

Christian Leadership Conference in Atlanta, Georgia.

Prior to their detention, the media asked Rev. Clark why the residents of Harris Neck did not resist the government's efforts to seize their property in 1942. He replied, "You have to consider the times (1942) when lynching was common. These people were also tense and scared to death, especially at the sight of men in military uniforms on their property. In those days if a white man brought you a death sentence paper, you signed it without question." By way of context, on July 25, 1946, two black couples were lynched near Moore's Ford Bridge in Walton County, Georgia. One of those killed was George W. Dorsey, who was a distinguished World War II veteran. He spent four years fighting for this country in the Pacific campaigns against the Japanese. None of those unjustly murdered had committed any crimes.

All four of the Harris Neck protestors were sentenced to 30 days in the county jail for trespassing. The Judge also immediately closed the refuge to the public, thus denying access to the watermen who depended on the Crabber's dock and boat ramps located on refuge lands. The presiding U.S. District Court Judge was Berry Avant Edenfield. Judge Edenfield had served in the Georgia State Senate and President Jimmy Carter nominated him to the United States District Court for the Southern District of Georgia in October 1978.

On November 17, 1979, the United States Court of Appeals, Fifth Circuit affirmed the misdemeanor convictions of Hercules Anderson, Ted Clark, Chris McIntosh and Edgar Timmons. In their decision, the judges opined, "Until the government's title (Harris Neck) is divested, the appellants must obey the process issued by the court system." They further stated, "The Marshall's guns were not drawn against the appellants, the militia was not called and those who chose to defy the court order were not injured. Even their confinement has been suspended pending this appeal."

While their guns may not have been drawn, the U.S. Marshalls arrived in the community with a huge contingent of law enforcement personnel. They didn't need the militia or National Guard to arrest four unarmed men, and since none of the accused had a criminal record, it is a normal practice for defendants to remain free pending the outcome of their appeal process.

It is also interesting there wasn't a single mention of where the defendants may have threatened a federal employee or caused any damage to the numerous fish and wildlife species living on the refuge. Just like Dr. Martin Luther King, Jr. and Mahatma Gandhi, these protestors were peaceful. The four community leaders ended up serving 15 days of confinement.

On August 25, 1980, Rev. Edgar Timmons, Jr. and POER filed a motion for relief seeking the return of Harris Neck. Less than a month later, Judge Edenfield denied the motion for relief and permanently enjoined the defendants from occupying Harris Neck. In his ruling, Edenfield noted, "Title is vested in the United States and cannot be returned to the original owners without Congressional authorization. There is no remedy for defendants in the courts."

Ironically, prior to this decision, FWS Project Leader, John Davis told the *Los Angeles Times*, "I'm not unsympathic with them and neither is the Department of the Interior. The legal questions are going to have to be resolved in the courts." Throughout the 80-year process of seeking justice for the former Harris Neck property owners and their heirs, there has been a lot of sympathy but a total lack of cooperation or willingness to obtain a "fair and equitable" solution.

On April 12, 1982, the United States Court of Appeals, Eleventh Circuit, issued its appeals ruling in the United States v. Timmons case. The court denied the appeal and affirmed the lower court's misguided decision to deny judicial relief to the former Harris Neck residents. The judges also ruled that the statute of limitation for any additional filings on the taking of this land had expired.

Without summarizing this ruling, it is shocking that this Appeals Court ignored the legal precedents of the landmark 1934 condemnation case, Olson v. United States, discussed earlier in chapter five. Though already mentioned, it is worth giving the Supreme Court's decision here again: "By the Fifth and Fourteenth Amendments of the Federal Constitution appropriation of private property for a public use is forbidden unless a full and exact equivalent be restored to the owner." Our highest court also opined that the owner of the condemned project should be placed, "In at least as good a position as if his property had not been taken." In the case of Harris Neck, their community and their way of life were destroyed, the people were left homeless and they received a pittance of compensation.

It is also distressing that the court declared that, "Harris Neck National Wildlife Refuge was then established by an Act of Congress in 1962. Public Law No. 80-537." This is factually wrong. P. L. 80-537 was a law enacted by the Congress in 1948. It authorized the "transfer of certain real property for wildlife or other purposes."

There is no mention of Harris Neck, Georgia in the law. In 1948, it was considered a military reservation. When it was given to McIntosh County, there was no intention to use the property for wildlife conservation but only for a commercial airport. There has never been a bill introduced, debated or enacted to establish the Harris Neck National Wildlife Refuge. There are 56 national wildlife refuges created by an Act of Congress and none of them mentions Harris Neck.

With the courthouse door seemingly closed to the people of Harris Neck, attention shifted to finding legislators willing to champion their righteous cause. On September 29, 1976, Congressman Bo Ginn, who represented Georgia's First Congressional District, introduced H.R. 15743. This bill called for the conveyance of Harris Neck lands back to those who owned them in 1942. The bill was referred to the House Judiciary Committee.

On May 9, 1979, Congressmen Bo Ginn and Reverend Walter Fauntroy, who represented the District of Columbia, introduced H.R. 4018. This legislation was referred to the House Merchant Marine and Fisheries Committee. Congressman

Ginn had been a member of that Committee for six years prior to his appointment to the House Appropriations Committee. The short title of the bill was: "To provide for the conveyance of lands comprising the Harris Neck Wildlife Refuge, McIntosh County, Georgia, to the persons, or the heirs of the persons who owned such land prior to the condemnation by the U.S. in 1943."

On that same day, Congressman Ginn wrote a letter to the Comptroller General of the United States, Elmer B. Staats. In his request, he asked, "I would like for your investigators (GAO) to determine if the original land acquisition was made in accordance with the law and if fair compensation was offered. I would further like to know if it can be established if verbal or written promises were made by an agent of the federal government regarding repurchase of the land, and, if so, whether such a promise constitutes a legally binding agreement at this time." In the United States, "Verbal agreements between two parties are just as enforceable as a written contract, so long as they do not violate the statue of Frauds."

Congressman Ginn also issued a press release about his new legislation, H.R. 4018. It said in part, "To permit the original owners of the Harris Neck Wildlife Refuge to repurchase their property, and has called for a federal investigation of the circumstances of the original acquisition of the land." Bo Ginn noted, "It will serve as a vehicle to fully develop the facts regarding the arrangement action of the government in seizing this property in the first place." In closing, Congressman Ginn stated, "If the facts show that the government took advantage of the original owners on the purchase price, then we should not expect the original owners to pay for that misdeed."

On June 22, 1979, U.S. Comptroller General Elmer Staats terminated Congressman Ginn's request. The official explanation offered was that it was the, "Policy of the Government Accounting Office not to investigate matters under litigation."

On December 7, 1979, the Merchant Marine and Fisheries Subcommittee on

Fisheries and Wildlife Conservation and the Environment conducted a hearing on H.R. 4018. This was 188 days since the arrest of the peaceful protestors in the Harris Neck National Wildlife Refuge. The Chairman of the Subcommittee was Congressman John Breaux of Crowley, Louisiana. In his opening statement, John Breaux said, "As I understand it, some of the original owners feel that the federal government has not dealt fairly with them concerning the 1943 condemnation actions. Apparently some landowners claim that government representatives promised that they could buy back the land after the U.S. Army had utilized it during the war."

In his testimony, Congressman Bo Ginn told the Subcommittee "I believe we in the Congress have a clear responsibility to explore allegations regarding Harris Neck. Upon a finding that the government was either directly or indirectly responsible for injustices. We have a mandate to correct them."

Congressman Walter E. Fauntroy opined in his statement to the Subcommittee, "If the government's agent told them they could reoccupy the land upon the war's end, the statement was good enough. The government, after all, was not going to renege upon its agents. Promises that were made to those, who were then displaced, unequal monies which were paid to blacks and whites for similar land, the lack of proper appraisals to determine the fair market value, and the demands for immediate departure - actually a demand resembling something more akin to an eviction than a departure and orderly move, cry out for Congressional intervention and rectification."

During the next three hours, the Subcommittee heard from a diverse group of 12 witnesses including Reverend Edgar Timmons, Jr., Evelyn Greer, Reverend Christopher McIntosh, Lynn Greenwalt, the Director of the U.S. Fish and Wildlife Service, The Honorable Thurnell Alston, who was the Acting Chairman of the McIntosh County Board of Commissioners and Hans Newhauser of the Georgia Conservancy.

Rev. Edgar Timmons, Jr. passionately told the Subcommittee, "We have been subjected to 37 years of oppression, suppression, and repression, under tremendous stress, but today we are still fighting for justice to reach out to Harris Neck. We often wonder why, why was it us, what did we do, to cause such a calamity? We have given our best. Our young men have served in our armies. We have died. We have bled. We are asking you gentlemen to consider this and please rectify this injustice."

Evelyn Greer, who was 15-year-olds when the federal government burned down her home, succinctly told the Subcommittee, "One afternoon, the government come in and this man came with a big bulldozer and he pushed over a tree and it fell over a part of our home and he came and said to my mother, 'Have you gotten everything out of your home?' She said only a few items left. 'He said, You have until 6'oclock in the morning.' We had worked all night back and forth, but that morning about 5'oclock, my mother and myself went, and when we got to where we could see our home, it was in flames. She (mother) said, we are on time but too late."

Rev. Christopher McIntosh testified, "I witnessed the bulldozer going into one of our graveyards (Thomas Cemetery) and push up the dead. And the bulldozer had a head under the tractor wheel. That cemetery was destroyed. I witnessed seeing a house going up into the air, black smoke shooting up in the air, being burned down because the people didn't get out in time enough."

He closed his statement, saying to the members of Congress, "If you all have heart in any shape or form, do something for us in this matter in the line of the United States, giving us justice, we really would appreciate it."

The Subcommittee then heard from the 7th Director of the U.S. Fish and Wildlife Service, Lynn Adams Greenwalt. He had been Director for eight years and was representing the views of the Carter Administration. Director Greenwalt told the members, "We are deeply concerned when charges are made that citizens have been treated unfairly or illegally. We believe that there is a need to seek the facts in this case."

Director Greenwalt then made two contradictory statements. He first said, "We do not support the approach taken in this bill that of the resale of federally required land at the original cost, particularly in the absence of specific proof of underpayment or discriminatory activity by federal employees or officials." This is an interesting position. The Fish and Wildlife Service obtained all of Harris Neck for free. More importantly, if he had taken the time to review the condemnation data that the War Department issued in 1945, he might have noticed that African Americans received $30,343 for 1,021 acres or $29.71 per acre, while the white landowners were paid $53,749 for 1,477 acres or $36.39 per acre. Clearly, there was a gross underpayment to the black property owners. The General Accounting Office would confirm these inequities in the 1985 report to the Congress.

Director Greenwalt then stated, "We prefer to withhold our recommendation on the preferable remedy." This was an incredibly disingenuous statement. Just seven months earlier, the FWS Realty Chief

Walter McAllister, who was responsible for buying private land for the refuge system, was quoted in the media as saying, "The Interior Department has no plans to return the wildlife property to the people who once lived there. It is a good refuge and we need it." Walter McAllister worked for Director Lynn Greenwalt.

The Subcommittee then heard from the Acting Chairman of the McIntosh County Board of Commissioners. Thurnell Alston told the Congressmen, "The evidence was very clear that this land was confiscated by the federal government under promises that it would be used only during the war period and would be sold back to the residents of Harris Neck at the end of the war and the existing national emergency. This promise was never kept."

One of the final witnesses was Hans Neuhausen, the Director of the Coastal Office of the Georgia Conservancy. According to its website, since its founding in 1967, "Georgia Conservancy and its members have ensured the protection and conservation of some of our state's most precious natural resources. Protecting Georgia through ecological and economic solutions for stewardship, conservation and sustainable use of the land and its resources."

In his testimony, Hans Neuhausen made three major points. First, he said, "Let me assure you that the Harris Neck issue is not a racial issue. At least half of the land acquired at Harris Neck by the U.S. government was owned by whites." Second, "The Georgia Conservancy is not aware of any evidence to support the claim that less than fair market value was paid to the original owners." Finally, "If there is any evidence of inappropriate action by the federal government, the nature of that compensation should be in money or lands of comparable value." Neuhausen told the members Harris Neck should never be returned to its previous owners and the Georgia Conservancy strongly opposed H.R. 4018.

President John Adams famously said, "Facts are stubborn things." Here are a few facts. Hans Neuhausen was born and raised in Boston, Massachusetts. He obtained his undergraduate degree at Middlebury College in Vermont. Since he didn't arrive in Georgia until 1964, he can be forgiven for probably not knowing about the long turbulent history of Harris Neck and the rampant racism that existed in the south for hundreds of years. Fortunately, there was not a lot of racism in either Massachusetts or Vermont.

Since its establishment in 1967, the Georgia Conservancy has had a warm relationship with both the State of Georgia and the U.S. Fish and Wildlife Service. As a member of the Georgia Land Trust, this coalition has as one of its key conservation missions to acquire hundreds of acres of private land for inclusion in national wildlife refuges and state parks.

Instead of just listening to his friends at FWS, Neuhausen should have contacted the U.S. Department of Defense and obtained a copy of their 1945 report entitled "Harris Neck Army Airfield, McIntosh County, Georgia, Acquisition Data." If he had read this document, he might have understood that the black landowners received neither fair market value nor compensation equal to what the white property owners received for their lands. There were no whites living in the community in 1942, each of them was an absentee property owner.

Sadly, this hearing was not well attended. Of the 30 members of the Subcommittee, only Chairman John Breaux, Ranking Republican Member Edwin B. Forsythe of New Jersey and Congressman Bill Hughes of New Jersey were in attendance. In response to a question from the Ranking Republican Member, Congressman Bo Ginn responded, "In this case, I just think the injustices are so clear that it is compelling. This land means something to these people. It was theirs and they lived on it and were happy on it, farming and fishing, and it is more than compensation. These people are the real preservationists and conservationists and environmentalists." Congressman Forsythe's response was, "I have great sympathy for your position but the real determination of equities here are a matter for the courts rather than Congress."

His colleague from the Garden State, Bill Hughes added, "I have only been here five years in the Congress but I think that your story is probably one of the most touching ones that I have heard and I am very sympathetic."

Before ending the hearing, Chairman John Breaux offered Congressman Ginn the opportunity for closing remarks. In his statement, Ginn noted, "There is no political mileage for me to take on people like Hans Newhauser and other groups. I simply believe a serious inequity existed at the time the property was reclassified. I believe an injustice was done to these people who love this land. It is their homeland and they want to return."

While Chairman Breaux indicated the Merchant Marine Committee would further investigate this issue, no further action was taken on this bill. What should have happened was for the Subcommittee to have a mark-up on H.R. 4018 and allow the members to vote Yea or Nay on the merits of this legislation. Sadly, this never occurred.

Ten days after the hearing in the House Merchant Marine and Fisheries Committee, Georgia's powerful senior Senator, Herman Tallmadge proposed S. 2143 for the relief of former Harris Neck residents. In those days, a U.S. Senator would introduce a bill and then submit a detailed explanation of the measure for *The Congressional Record*. For whatever reason, Senator Talmadge decided to forgo this procedure. There is not a single word of explanation about the purposes of his legislation. There were no hearings or any action on S. 2143. It is interesting to note that before his election to the U.S. House of Representatives, Bo Ginn had served as the Chief of Staff for Senator Talmadge. Was the Senate bill introduced as a favor to his former Chief of Staff?

On July 31, 1980, Congressmen Bo Ginn and Walter Fauntroy introduced H.R. 7897. This was a private relief bill for the former residents and their heirs who had lived in Harris Neck. The same legislation was reintroduced in the 97th Congress as H.R. 1044 on January 22, 1981. Both of these measures were referred to the House Judiciary Committee and no legislative action was ever taken. At that time, the Chairman of the Judiciary Committee was Congressman Peter Rodino of Newark, New Jersey. He represented the 10th District that had a majority black constituency. In his May 8, 2005 obituary, Chairman Rodino was described this way, "He had compiled a liberal voting record, and pushed hard for civil rights and immigration reform." Sadly, he didn't push the passage of the Harris Neck relief bills endorsed by the Emergency Land Fund, McIntosh County Board of Commissioners, NAACP and the Southern Christian Leadership Conference.

In 1983, Congressman Ronald "Bo" Ginn left the House of Representatives after unsuccessfully running for the Democratic nomination for the Governor of Georgia. I suspect there were many reasons why his legislation was never enacted into law. These include: members of Congress felt the courts should decide this case, racism, the strong opposition of the federal government to any solution, unwillingness to stand up for justice for a small group of Americans living in rural Georgia, and the Harris Neck movement simply lacked the funds to hire expensive lobbyists who would plead their case on Capitol Hill. It is interesting that not a single one of Congressman Ginn's colleagues in the Georgia House delegation ever added their name as a co-sponsor of these important bills. Perhaps they were never asked.

It is now more than 40 years later and no additional federal bills have been introduced to correct this blatant injustice. The current representative of the 1st Congressional District in Georgia, Buddy Carter has indicated he has no interest in taking up the cause of the Harris Neck Land Trust.

Chapter 7 and Chapter 8 was written by co-author David Kelly.

Chapter 7: Birth of the Harris Neck Land Trust

Sometime in the spring of 2000, I was driving back to my home in the Sierra Mountain foothills, east of Sacramento from my sister's house near San Francisco. I turned on the radio and searched for the local *NPR* station to hear the day's news, and there was Steve Kurwood's voice, introducing *NPR's* weekly environmental news segment, *Living on Earth*. I had not heard this show in quite some time because it was not carried on my local *NPR* station.

I was very familiar with this program because my own radio program *Our Sustainable Future* was in competition with *LOI* in the early 1990s. Both of us trying to sell our programs to National Public Radio and hoping to get syndicated across *NPR's* vast American network of affiliate stations. *LOI* had succeeded.

Beginning in Cambridge, MA *LOI* was now on the air across much of *NPR's* network. Today's segment was titled: "Georgia Lost and Found." Kurwood introduced the listening audience to Jesse Wegman, the free-lance journalist who had gone to coastal Georgia to report on the story. It was the story of Harris Neck and Wegman's only guest was 58-year-old Wilson Moran.

As I drove through Contra Costa County, I listened to Wilson talk, as he and Wegman drove through the Harris Neck National Wildlife Refuge in Wilson's squeaky old Chevy pickup truck. Wilson spoke movingly about what life had been like in Harris Neck. He spoke of his beloved grandfather, Robert Dawley, and how much of life he had learned from this wise, old fisherman; he spoke with reverence of the land and the waters and the beauty of Harris Neck; and he spoke of the loss and the pain his grandfather, and other elders, suffered when they were forced off their land.

He said his grandfather, who had been a successful businessman, had never really recovered from the taking of Harris Neck and how the taking was done. Robert Dawley, who raised Wilson, died in 1960 when Wilson was seventeen. Graduating from high school later that year and seeing no opportunities for himself, as a black man in McIntosh County, Wilson joined the Army.

I had never heard of Harris Neck before that day in 2000, and had my sister not called and invited me for a visit that weekend, and had I not turned on the radio just when I did, I, most likely, never would have. Perhaps my life in California would have gone forward there for many years, but it didn't. Without knowing it that day, my life was about to change in a big way and remain changed forever.

This was the first, of many, serendipitous events that would continue for the next 22 years in connection with Harris Neck. As I got to know many of the people in Harris Neck, with their strong Baptist faith, I discovered they viewed my hearing about Harris Neck, and the other unusual events that followed, not as serendipity but as something more divinely directed.

I was intrigued from the start by the story of Harris Neck. Who knows what draws a person to one story and not another? This one pulled me in, at a visceral level, from the very beginning. It was as though I could feel the beauty of the land and waters as Wilson described them, and I could feel the importance of Harris Neck for him and, most assuredly, for his elders.

The next day, I called *Living on Earth* and they gave me Jesse Wegman's phone number. I called him and introduced myself and my interest in the excellent interview he had done with Wilson. He said he was just placing a CD of the program and a letter in an envelope addressed to Wilson when his phone rang. I asked him if he would include my name and phone number in the package. He said he would. He also said his interview with Wilson just scratched the surface of what he described as "a huge, intriguing and complex story."

Two weeks later, there was a message on my answering machine from Wilson Moran. Before I even took off my work clothes, I called the number he left. It was the first of many calls I would make to Wilson over the next several months. I started researching anything and everything connected with Harris Neck – the Middle Passage and the slave trade into Charleston, SC and later Savannah, GA; plantation life in Georgia; eminent domain; US Army bases in the southeast; the Gullah Geechee culture, or what little I could find on it then, and much more.

The research was fascinating, but I was limited doing it from afar with only my local library and the burgeoning Internet available to me. During perhaps my twentieth call to Wilson, he simply said, "Dave Kelly, you want to know more? Fly to Atlanta, rent a car and drive toward Savannah. Go south on Interstate 95 and take exit 67. Turn left, go to the Shell station and call me." I laughed and asked him for the name of a local motel. He said I didn't need one.

A month later, having arranged time off at work, I followed Wilson's instructions. I had not been waiting long at the Shell station, when Wilson arrived in his squeaky but sound 1970s-vintage, pickup. After the briefest of hellos, I followed him east on Harris Neck Road toward the ocean. Just as I started to smell the sea, Wilson turned into the driveway of his nicely kept, modest home. He introduced me to his lovely wife, Ernestine and the three of us sat down to a wonderful dinner of shrimp and rice, collard greens, cornbread and ice tea. I immediately felt at home. Their graciousness and hospitality reminded me of my mother's, and the food was delicious.

Wilson and I sat up late that first night on his small, screened, back porch, and we talked about many things. I took an immediate liking to this gregarious and rather charismatic man. For the entire week I stayed with the Moran's, we were up early every day for a fine, big breakfast and then off to meet Wilson's relatives and scores of friends and acquaintances, black and white. He seemed to know everyone in the county and every other black man or woman we met was a cousin.

The first thing we did, however, on that first morning after breakfast, was drive through the Harris Neck homeland, aka Harris Neck National Wildlife Refuge. The entrance to the refuge was not more than a mile from Wilson and Ernestine's house. The Moran's, his parents, who lived next door, and many other families from Harris Neck had found parcels of land close to their homeland, following the advice of Army officers in 1942 to "not move far away." Passing over Julienton Creek, Wilson turned into the refuge. We drove through a tunnel of magnificent live oaks, dripping with Spanish moss. They were standing as if sentinels of the past.

Wilson explained that there were once hundreds of these beautiful, old trees spread all across Harris Neck but that Sherriff Poppell had most of them cut down for their valuable timber after the county acquired the land in the late '40s. Wilson and I soon passed a somewhat dilapidated large brick barn and two small trailer homes. These were the only three buildings on the 2,824 acres of Harris Neck when I first visited in 2000. There was virtually no signage for anything, except the six or seven ponds, including the main Woody Pond that Fish and Wildlife had created. The refuge was all woodlands, meadows and marsh.

We parked near Woody Pond and got out to walk along the berm at the south end. Since it was mid-summer, there were not many wood storks to be seen, but Wilson did point out two as they flew overhead. In the air they look quite beautiful; not so much up close, with their vulture-like heads. I did see some large blue herons and several egrets, and there were lots of ducks and young alligators sunbathing on logs in the shallow waters of the pond. Wilson passed me his binoculars and pointed to one of the several tiny islands in the large pond. It was the largest alligator I had ever seen, and, as I panned this and the other islands, I saw many gators that looked to be longer than 12 feet. As much as I loved to swim, I would not be doing so here.

As we drove through the refuge, Wilson's voice was soft and slow. I realized this was painful for him to be driving through the land his ancestors had toiled on as slaves, sunup till sundown, six days-a-week, as far back as the mid-to-late 1700s, land that his grandfather had farmed as a free men and then passed on to his own parents.

"I don't like to coming here," Wilson said as he stopped at the end of one of the Army airfield runways. I said we could go back to his house, but he said, "No, it's okay; you need to see this. My people owned all of this. They farmed and hunted on this land. Their blood, sweat, tears, hopes and dreams are in this soil. They fished and oystered and crabbed. They had it all. As my mom would say, "'It was a hard life, but it was a good life.'"

Later that day, Wilson and I set out in his 18-foot skiff from the only boat ramp on the refuge. This was Barbour River Landing. We motored out Barbour River, through the estuary, toward the Atlantic Ocean. Dolphins swam close alongside or could be seen not far away, fishing in small pods. Since my first close encounter with them as a little boy in a small boat off the west coast of Florida, where my dad had taken his young family one Easter, I always felt a special kinship with them. These fascinating mammals, which Wilson said, his people call the fishermen. Wilson cut the engine and we drifted. He picked up his net and made a beautiful circular cast. Moments later he pulled it up and emptied two dozen shrimp into the boat. I had never even seen a cast net before, let alone someone handling one so effortlessly.

When I asked him how old he was when he learned to cast a net, he told me of the time his grandfather first taught him at age seven. This funny story had Wilson following the net into the water more than once. He told me many stories about his grandfather that afternoon and evening. He told of how he knew, many hours or even a day before, when a storm was coming; of how his ancestors were taken from Sierra Leone for their rice-growing knowledge; of how the flooding of the rice fields was controlled by the tides; and of how he carefully managed his life and his business dealings in white controlled McIntosh County.

That wonderful week ended too soon. The night before I left to drive to Atlanta and catch my flight to Sacramento, Wilson told Ernestine we were going down to the river. First, however, we drove to the nearest package store and bought two cigars and a six-pack of Heineken. As a Baptist, he was not supposed to drink or smoke but I already knew Wilson did not abide by all the rules. We went to Barbour River and sat on the boat landing, just above the water's edge. We sat in the bright moonlight on a night with enough breeze to keep the annoying gnats at bay. "Are you going to come back?" Wilson queried, softly. I said I would be back, but I felt Wilson was not sure I would return. Then, a few dolphins could be heard, surfacing. I saw the moonlight glistening off the backs of two, then three, and then four of them. Wilson said, "They've come to say goodbye." What a gift that was.

I had come to McIntosh County and to Harris Neck to meet Wilson and others to get a feel for some of the personal dimensions of this story. Driving to Atlanta the next morning, I took as many back roads as I possibly could. Georgia was a state of about 15 million people in 2001. About half the population lived in metro-Atlanta. Driving past cotton fields and huge groves of pecan and walnut trees and then through several lovely small towns, I knew I had to come back and I realized I needed to do some serious research in the Savannah Historical Society, the National Archives' regional center outside Atlanta, and other archives and museums.

It was only a matter of days back in California that I felt a pressing need to know so much more about Harris Neck, not only the history and the facts of the taking, but more about the people and the life they had lived before the 1940s and the one they now have. I had met many people who grew up on the land, including some who were in their twenties and thirties at the time of the taking - people who were there when the terrible deed was done. I needed to get to know them and hear their stories. How was I going to do this, living on the other side of the country?

At this time, I had already started writing a book based on many of the interviews I had done during the two years I had my radio program on the air. In fact, I had recently taken a train to Colorado to meet with and interview the wonderful writer and Native American rights activist, Vine Deloria. I had wanted to interview him for *Our Sustainable Future* but never got the opportunity and I wanted to add his and a few other new interviews to the book. It would not be easy putting that project on the shelf, but I started to think I may soon be doing just that.

A few months later and after many more calls with Wilson, I asked my boss for two-week's vacation. He wasn't thrilled, but he said yes. I flew back to Atlanta, where I spent three days in the National Archives, looking through several thousand pages of documents on the taking of Harris Neck. I also went to the Georgia Department of Archives and History, where I found a copy of Margret Ann Harris' Last Will and Testament. This was another serendipitous event.

No one had told me I could possibly find anything in particular on Harris Neck at this archive. This document was not on my mind, since I didn't even know of its existence. I was actually looking for something more on the Army airfield, when I saw Margret Harris's name slide by on the microfilm machine. It was an exhilarating feeling, finding this important document written 135 years earlier – a document written by a free black man, Tunis Campbell. His signature is the only one on Harris' will; she and the other witnesses had made their marks with an X. Campbell, who was raised not far from where I was in New Jersey, worked for the newly created Freedmen's Bureau and was Commissioner for this Bureau on St. Catherine's Island, just off the coast of Harris Neck.

When I called Wilson and told him of my find, he was very excited but also surprised because, unbeknownst to me, the McIntosh County Courthouse had burned down three times, twice under very suspicious circumstances. How, he wondered, had this document survived? The only explanation we came up with was that Tunis Campbell had also recorded the document in Liberty County, just north of McIntosh, because St. Catherine's Island was part of Liberty.

The next day I drove to Savannah to spend time in the Savannah Historical Society. After two days there, I drove an hour down the coast to McIntosh County, got a room in the lovely Open Gates B&B in Darien, and spent most of my second week with Wilson and several of the Harris Neck elders, including and especially, Wilson's gracious and wonderful story-telling mother, Mary Dawley Moran. I also met many of the other elders, including Wilson's father, Roosevelt, Evelyn Greer, Olive Smith and her 101-year-old mother, Ophelia, the Reverend Robert Thorpe, Kenneth Dunham, Alonza Campbell and Chris McIntosh, Sr.

I liked each and every one of the elders, and over the coming years I grew to have a fondness for them that I never had and still don't feel – for the most part – for their first-generation descendants, those of Wilson's generation. Of these younger folks, I met Rev. Edgar Timmons, Hercules Anderson, Chris McIntosh, Jr., Olive Hillery, Olive Smith's daughter, and many others.

The elders, all but one who, at this writing, are now gone, seemed to possess something that the next generation does not have. I am not sure what that is, and it may be more than one thing. Was it their intimate connection to the land? Was it their closer ties to their ancestors, and the resulting deep authenticity of the lives they led on Harris Neck? Was it some profound sense of their humility and their deeply rooted place on this earth that gave them a much more positive outlook than their children seem to have? Or was it the hard, daily physical work in a much cleaner environment, where all the food they ate and water they drank was free of chemicals of any kind? Were they simply healthier – in body and soul?

It was an eye-opening journey - those two weeks. I had stepped into another culture, one I had known absolutely nothing about just months earlier. On the plane back to Sacramento, I felt overwhelmed by the experience, but it was a good feeling – a mix of fulfillment and excitement and new possibilities. Getting back home, I put my other writing project on the shelf and started to review the two journals-full of notes from my trip and the more than 200 pages of documents I had copied from the different archives and historical societies I had visited.

Over the next several months, I struggled to write a story about Harris Neck. I saw it as a book. I tried to keep my phone calls to Wilson to a minimum, but I don't think I was very successful. I began to feel this project was too much for me, that I had bitten off much more than I could chew. I put it down, I picked it up, I put it down again.

Then, one morning I turned on the TV and saw a plane crash into the World Trade Center, the building where I had worked in the 1980s. My girlfriend and I sat and watched as millions of others did. She and I eventually finished getting dressed and went to work, though neither of us did anything there except watch TV or listen to the radio. That night I felt something basic shift in me – an awareness of my own mortality, for sure, but also something else, some need for a different way of living or a different way of seeing the life I was living. Harris Neck pulled at me again.

Two weeks later, I gave my notice at work and had a long talk with my girlfriend. I told her I thought it would take me nine to twelve months to write this book. She asked how I would live. She asked if she could visit. Of course, I said. By late October, I had packed my car and started the drive across the country. My first week in McIntosh was spent at the same B&B, and then I moved into a lovely, small cottage near the water. If I couldn't write the book in this quiet and idyllic setting, then I just did not have the talent.

Months passed, writing and not writing. I continued meeting and spending more time with many people from Harris Neck. I spent lots of time with Wilson, and he and Ernestine had me over for Sunday dinner on a fairly regular basis. I also started to get to know Rev. Edgar Timmons, the pastor of First African Baptist Church of Harris Neck. He and Wilson and I took some day trips together to visit others from Harris Neck, who lived in Savannah or other towns in Georgia, Florida or South Carolina. My knowledge of Harris Neck and its people was deepening and broadening but early in 2002 I stopped writing. I just could not figure out the story I wanted to tell. It just felt too big for me.

In the meantime, and through Wilson, of course, I met John Littles, the young, black, executive director of a fairly new community-based non-profit called McIntosh Sustainable Environment and Economic Development or McIntosh SEED or McSEED for short. To my understanding, this was the first organization in the county's long history that brought together blacks and whites to discuss issues of common concern, such as affordable housing, environmental preservation, education and tourism.

One thing led to another, and I was soon hired by John as McSEED's project coordinator. This opened up things for me even more, and I got to know many new people – educators, county officials, other activists along the coast and politicians.

I told Wilson I had stopped writing. He was upset. He wanted the story to be told and to reach a larger audience and he wanted to be part of the whole thing. He said I had a golden opportunity, like no other, and that I was squandering it. I can't recall now what I told him, except that I guess I just didn't have the talent. But we continued to see each other. He went out on the river every chance he could get and I went with him rather often. He was also a very active Board member of McSEED and he and John

Littles and I spent a lot of time talking about the issues confronting the county's development. We also traveled together to various conferences as representatives of McSEED.

Instead of writing, I got very involved in the activities of McSEED, and perhaps naively believed that the white people involved with McSEED, especially the whites on the Board, would continue to work closely and openly with this grassroots organization, headed by a young black man. I started meeting local politicians and some state and national leaders. I also began working with other environmental groups and I met staff of the foundations that started supporting McIntosh SEED.

As McSEED grew and started getting some good media attention, other foundations started noticing the work we were doing. Some very important foundations, such as The Mary Reynolds Babcock Foundation, started awarding us grants. Though I was very busy and also not writing about Harris Neck, it and its people were never far from my mind.

With the work I was doing with McSEED and the wide variety of people and organizations I was becoming exposed to, I kept thinking about possible connections to Harris Neck. I also read more about the community's first organized movement to reclaim the land that started in the late 1970's, and I talked more with the leaders of that movement. I also started learning more about the Gullah or Gullah Geechee culture and I began to realize the important connection between this culture, which the people of Harris Neck are part of, and the land of Harris Neck. I saw the all-important connection between cultural/historic preservation and environmental preservation, and I realized that no culture had a stronger ethic of environmental preservation than the Gullah Geechee.

I had some limited knowledge at the time of land trusts, and one day I picked up the phone and called the national headquarters of The Trust for Public Lands (TPL) in San Francisco. I asked if they had anyone who dealt with issues in the Georgia or South Carolina low country. They gave me the phone number of Russ Marane who worked for TPL in Bluffton, SC. My thought was that Congress, which is where I understood any possible resolution for Harris Neck lay, would not want to deal with seventy-odd families. Harris Neck would need a single, legally constituted entity that represented all the families and all the descendants of Harris Neck.

I introduced myself to Russ and briefly told him about Harris Neck and my idea about how we might get a second movement off the ground by forming a land trust. Russ was gracious enough to set up a meeting with Wilson and me for the next week in Savannah. I then drove up to see Wilson who was working in his garden. While helping him pull carrots and onions, I told him of the idea and my call with Russ.

The following Friday, Wilson and I met Russ at a Denny's for a two-hour breakfast. Russ had an exciting and important resume, including a high-profile job with President Carter's administration. He liked our approach with the land trust and he was most informative about how to set one up and how we might move forward with the entire concept. He knew a little about Harris Neck and a lot about U.S. Fish and Wildlife. He gave us many cautions about this agency and gave us some good direction about the entire political process. He said, even though a resolution would be through an Act of Congress, we needed to make sure we started at the local level.

He said we should meet with the McIntosh Board of County Commissioners to let them know our plans and to get their blessing. He also said before going to Congress, we needed to eliminate every conceivable objection they could have for righting this wrong and returning the land to its rightful owners. He said this would not be easy, not at all, but that it was possible. It would take time and a lot of thoughtful planning and hard work.

By the time we finished two pots of coffee, we seemed to feel very comfortable with each other. Russ asked if we had a name for the organization. We said, simply the Harris Neck Land Trust. Russ said he would speak with an attorney friend and ask if he would help incorporate us with the Georgia Secretary of State. After meeting with Russ, Wilson and I set up a meeting with Rev. Robert Thorpe and Pastor Edgar Timmons to lay out our concept and talk about the meeting we just had. They liked the whole idea and plan, and two weeks later, the four of us met with Russ Marane and Austin Catts, an attorney in Brunswick, GA. Austin knew about Harris Neck and liked what he heard about our plan. He advised us to set up the Trust as an LLC and not as a 501 C 3 non-profit, so that individuals on the Board of Directors would not have any financial liabilities.

A few weeks later, we received our incorporation papers from the Georgia Secretary of State. Though we did not yet have an office or a Board of Directors, it was now official – the Harris Neck Land Trust was the legally incorporated entity that would lead the new Harris Neck Justice Movement. Austin Catts did not charge us for his legal advice or his incorporation work.

At 6:00 PM on December 12, 2005, the Harris Neck Land Trust held its first monthly meeting at First AB Church of Harris Neck. Russ Marane and Austin Catts joined perhaps ninety Harris Neck elders and descendants for what turned out to be a long, spirited meeting.

Wilson and Pastor Timmons had gotten the word out about this meeting. Most of those in attendance knew nothing about the Trust or the plans to reclaim Harris Neck. Some who came to the church that evening was very excited and vocal, thinking the land was being returned, and they wanted to know if they were going to get their parents or grandparents land back for themselves. Most others anxiously listened to what Wilson, Pastor Timmons and Rev. Thorpe laid out as calmly as they could.

The meeting began with a long prayer, thanking God for the day, praising him, and asking for his guidance in keeping everyone on one accord and in good faith as we started down the road before us. Rev. Thorpe said this journey would not be easy and that we all needed patience and strength and faith to see it through. After some time and through a fair amount of confusion where Austin

Catts and Russ Marane tried to provide the necessary legal information and why the Land Trust had been set up in the first place, the assemblage, not all of which was satisfied, got down to the business of choosing a Board of Directors and an Executive Committee.

When that was done, with quite a bit of excited discussion, Rev. Thorpe and Olive Hillery, the newly appointed Board Chair and Secretary took their rightful places at the head of the gathering. Rev. Thorpe, who I would very soon see was a natural leader and the best choice for the Trust's first Chair, told the gathering that the Trust would proceed as a single body, representing every family from Harris Neck.

With that in mind, he said the Trust needed to locate every family from Harris Neck and that each family needed to choose, a single representative to the Trust. This produced a fair amount of excited discussion in the large gathering. Rev. Thorpe let the mild uproar continue for a few beats and then reined things in with the suggestion that the next and immediate order of business should be the formation of a Family Representative Committee that would search for all the Harris Neck families.

Rev. Thorpe then introduced me and said that I had completed a good deal of research into the taking of Harris Neck and the first movement to try to reclaim the land. I was still unknown to many of those I stood to address, and being an outsider, and white, I was not trusted by anyone who had not already gotten to know me. That was everyone except Wilson, his mother Mary, Pastor Timmons and Rev. Thorp.

I briefly introduced myself and said how I came to be living in McIntosh County, the work I was doing with McSEED and the research I had done, especially at the National Archives. And with that, I unrolled the map of Harris Neck made by the U. S. War Department in 1945, that I had taken from the National Archives. It was too large for copying at the Archives, which had allowed me to copy any and all documents I wanted, and since I thought it was needed by the community and that it really belonged to those from Harris Neck, I took it.

The map listed each and every tract of land, all 171 of them, and gave the name of the owner and the number of acres in each tract. This was the perfect starting place for the Family Rep Committee. I said I would make a copy for each committee member and for anyone else who wanted a copy. I had already given copies to Wilson and a few others. Everyone raised their hand for a copy.

It was then decided that the Trust would meet at 6:30 PM on the second Monday of every month at the church. With that and a surprising amount of a work having been completed, Rev. Thorpe asked Pastor Timmons to lead the gathering in a closing prayer. The prayer concluded, Rev. Thorpe asked for a motion and a second to adjourn the first meeting of the Harris Neck Land Trust.

That done the church seemed to almost erupt with joyful greetings among relations and neighbors, those who had come from Savannah or other more distance locales, and those who had not seen each other in years. Men and women shook hands or hugged each other, excitedly. People mingled for the longest time, moving from one person or group to another. It was a joyful end to a long, sometimes difficult, meeting. We had taken the first step on a new, mostly - unchartered journey; we had no idea how long a journey it would be.

The next several months were spent finding all the families, having each family choose a representative, setting up committees, writing Bylaws and forming an Advisory Board. I continued doing research, and I set out to find an eminent domain attorney and then the best people we could attract and ask to be members of our Advisory Board. Rev. Thorpe and I talked about this and agreed we needed to find the best person available, in several key areas, starting with our specific need and then trying to fill the position.

I did the research and then talked with Rev. Thorpe about each candidate. He then extended the invitations. Since Russ Marane had already proved so valuable and since his range of experience was so broad and deep and his connections seemed to be endless, we agreed that he would be our first ask. Thankfully, he accepted.

We needed someone to help us navigate Capitol Hill. I asked my older brother, who was then the lead attorney for NIKE and who worked closely with NIKE's DC office, for suggestions. He said he didn't need to look further than their DC office and a man named Orson Porter.

Orson is a brilliant, soft-spoken and unflappable black man, who seemed to know just about everyone on Capitol Hill. He was also well connected to the Congressional Black Caucus. We knew we would need their help. Orson accepted when we asked and almost immediately he proved helpful.

Next, I discovered Kathleen Cleaver, the former Black Panther and former wife of the late Eldridge Cleaver, was teaching law at both Emory University and Yale University. When I mentioned her name to Rev. Thorpe, he was dubious, at first, because of her association with the Black Panthers, which had a mixed reputation in both the black and white community. However, when he and I talked at some length about her legal expertise (she had received a law degree from Yale after leaving the Panthers), her civil rights work and her other activist associations, Thorpe asked me to approach her. She, too, graciously accepted and soon started opening other doors for us.

Then came Dr. Emory Campbell, a black scholar and historian, a former director of the Penn Center in South Carolina, and a man of Gullah descent. Emory's connections were also extensive. Dr. Campbell would also soon become the first Executive Director of the newly established Gullah Geechee Cultural Heritage Corridor Commission. Congress had authorized this commission in 2006 for the purposes of preserving the Gullah Geechee culture and creating a heritage and cultural corridor from North Carolina to northern Florida to celebrate and communicate this unique culture.

Al Williams, the first black State Representative from coastal Georgia; Norman Hill, President Emeritus of the A.

Philip Randolph Institute; and Edward "Jerry" Pennick, Director of the Land Assistance Fund for the very important Federation of Southern Cooperatives, were also invited to serve on the Trust's Advisory Board. All three gentlemen accepted. Jerry Pennick was very familiar with Harris Neck and had been an integral part of the first movement as Director of the Emergency Land Fund.

Rev. Edgar Timmons was also named to the Board as a spiritual advisor and because of his intimate knowledge of the first movement. In fact, he was one of four men, who were jailed briefly in Savannah for their civil disobedience and participation in the Tent-In in 1979 that protested U.S. Fish and Wildlife Service's occupation of Harris Neck.

Last but not least, and somewhat later, Dr. Norm Kurland, President of the Center for Economic and Social Justice in Washington, DC also joined the Advisory Board. CESJ was a prestigious group and several members would prove invaluable to the Trust for their connections, the closed doors they were able to open for us, the counsel they provided and for their overall support and encouragement.

With regard to our search for an eminent domain attorney, we found Dan Beirsdorf of Beirsdorf and Associates in Minneapolis, Minnesota. Eminent domain law is his bread and butter and we could not have found a better attorney for our specific needs. With a couple of phone calls, he took me through the law and then sent me a list of all the violations of the people's Fourth and Fifteenth Amendment rights committed by the War Department in its application of eminent domain in 1942. Dan refused to charge us for his time and expertise.

Rev. Robert Thorpe, whose family called Robbie, was a strongly built and imposing man. Born in Harris Neck in 1931, he had lost his parents at a young age. Robert Dawley raised Robbie, who grew up alongside his older cousin, Mary Dawley Moran. In his younger days, he had been a stevedore on the Savannah docks and now was the Pastor of Savannah's Peaceful Zion Church. I liked Rev. Thorpe from the first, and would later find him to be an honest, honorable and hard-working man, who was devoted to his lovely wife, Mildred, and who was passionate about the Harris Neck fight for justice.

Once the Trust was formed, Rev. Thorpe and I started seeing more of each other. With and without the rest of the Harris Neck Board, I had several lunches and dinners at the Thorpe's lovely home in Savannah. Outside of formal meetings, I was soon just calling him Rev. We were both huge baseball fans and would go to watch the Savannah Sand Gnats, a farm team for the New York Mets, at nearby Grayson Stadium. It was such a treat, seeing good baseball in this intimate stadium, which seated about 7,000, for $5 a ticket, and we always had great seats. Rev. also took me fishing off the coast of Savannah in one of his two boats. I have never been much of a fisherman, but this was one of Rev. Thorpe's passions, and I always enjoyed our time on the water. We talked about Harris Neck, baseball and life in general and soon we became good friends.

At some point in 2006, after a dinner with Rev. and Mrs. Thorpe, he asked me to be the Trust's Project Coordinator. Though everyone contributed financially at the monthly community meetings, the Trust did not have the funds to pay me or anyone else, but I was working for McIntosh SEED and doing a little consulting for other community groups on the Georgia coast. I humbly accepted the volunteer position.

With 2006 spent organizing and developing the Trust, refining our Mission and Objectives, setting up committees, training the Board of Directors, pulling together the Advisory Board and getting some local media attention, we were ready to put the Harris Neck Justice Movement into second gear. On January 9, 2007 at the New Year's very first meeting of the McIntosh County Board of Commissioners, the Trust's Board of Directors and dozens of Harris Neck elders and descendants took their seats in the Commissions chambers. We had all arrived early and taken two-thirds of the seats, so that the large crowd of county residents ended up overflowing into the hallway. The meeting was videotaped and there was a lot of excitement in the air in that crowded room.

The Harris Neck Land Trust was not the first item on the Commission's agenda. But after calling the meeting to order, Boyd Gault, Commissioner-at-Large moved the Trust up to the first order of business, stating that, "It looks as though most of you are here concerning Harris Neck, so we will begin with the reading of the Harris Neck Resolution by Wilson Moran."

Wilson, Rev. Thorpe and I had already met individually with each of the five commissioners in December to inform them of the Resolution we had written and to answer their questions about the Trust and our plans. We felt sure of four votes and thought we had the fifth as well.

Mr. Gault was one of the first people I had met when I moved to McIntosh County – one of the few not introduced to me by Wilson Moran. I met Boyd, who I later discovered was well respected and liked by those from Harris Neck, at a small café called Jakes's, a block away from Open Gates B&B. We had breakfast together several times, and I found him to be an honest and likeable man.

Wilson walked up to the microphone, positioned ten feet in front of the table where the five Commissioners, the County Attorney and the County Clerk sat facing the assemblage. Wilson read the three-page document, which we had intentionally worded rather strongly, each member of the commission reading along from their own copies. When Wilson finished and took his seat, Mr. Gault simply asked for a show of hands on the Resolution. It was unanimous. The County Attorney, however, asked that the Resolution be tabled for his further review and discussion with the commissioners, saying he had not even been born at the time of the taking and was not sure of the veracity of everything in the Resolution.

To that and without hesitation, the Rev. Nathaniel Grovner, one of the two black commissioners, said, "Well, I was there, and what you have heard, and a lot more, is true." The other black commissioner, Charles Jordan voiced his agreement with Grovner, and Boyd Gault simply said, "We have unanimous agreement, and the Resolution is hereby passed." The chamber erupted in applause, many patting Wilson on the back.

Everyone from Harris Neck then exited the room and the commission continued with its business. The hallway was now very crowded and noisy; people from Harris Neck were happily shaking hands and embracing one another, while other Harris Neck supporters were wishing them well. There were at least two representatives of the media standing with microphones or tape recorders. Kathleen Russell, editor of *The Darien News* interviewed Wilson, and *Georgia Public Broadcasting's* Orlando Montoya introduced himself to me.

We had taken our first political step, and it was an important one, establishing the support of our own county commission. Among other things, the Harris Neck Resolution acknowledged the County's complicity in the acquisition of Harris Neck after World War II and the numerous violations by the county in its contract with the federal government from 1948 to 1961. The Commission also recognized the Trust as the legal entity pursuing the return of Harris Neck to its rightful owners and stated its support of the Trust.

At the next several regular community meetings, we started talking about what we wanted the new Harris Neck to look like. Rev. Thorpe, who had known the original community intimately, gave some good advice. He said we should not try to re-create the old Harris Neck. We should take our community, environmental ethics and our Christian ideals and build a modern Harris Neck based on these things and the way the elders had lived on Harris Neck.

I had been doing research into companies that could help with our plans and with Russ Marane's contacts, the Trust hired a landscape architecture and land use planning firm out of Atlanta. JB+A knew our funds were limited, but they took the work, and we were soon able to start paying them with a portion of a grant I had written for McSEED that was able to come to the Trust.

While JB+A was assisting us with our Preservation and Community

Development Plan, through a series of meetings with the Board and community members, we also contracted a natural resources consulting firm to conduct environmental and cultural/historic assessments of Harris Neck. These assessments and inventories were then incorporated into our Preservation and Community Development Plan. At that time, the Trust was seeking the return of all the land of Harris Neck, so the development plan was quite comprehensive and perhaps a bit overwhelming to outsiders who had seen it. Opposition to the Trust and our plans was soon voiced in the county, and pushback began from some citizens and staff at the refuge.

The Harris Neck Justice Movement began as a transparent and completely democratic and inclusive organization, and those ideals have remained intact up to the present. In the beginning, in addition to our search for all the Harris Neck families, the Trust also reached out to the white families who had owned land on Harris Neck. This movement was for everyone, black and white. Folks from a few of the white families came to a community meeting or two in 2006, but for whatever reasons, they stopped coming. One family that came to several meetings was the Thorpe family. Isabel Thorpe Mealing, born in 1907, was the daughter of E. M. Thorpe. Isabel, who lived in Darien, and her daughter Katherine, who lived in Alabama, attended a few meetings but they also lost interest after some time.

With some grant writing experience from my earlier life with a non-profit in New York, I started researching foundations and other organizations that I thought might be interested in funding the Trust. Since the Trust had been formed as a LLC and not as a 501 C 3 non-profit, it could not accept grant funds directly. We would need a fiscal agent. The choice for me was very logical – the Federation of Southern Cooperatives. This organization, based in Atlanta, had been very supportive of the first Harris Neck movement. Jerry Pennick, who assisted the Harris Neck group, the People Organized for Equal Rights, twenty-five years earlier, was still with the Federation, which had been established in 1967 with the mission of helping preserve family farms, especially those that were black owned and in the southeast.

When I approached the Federation, they were happy to act as our fiscal agent, and they refused to even take the small percentage of the grants we hoped to receive, as was the normal practice of fiscal agents (to cover their administrative costs). They believed wholeheartedly in our mission and were happy a new movement had begun. Their support has never wavered and they have provided good contacts and advice along the way.

Much seems to be made of the art, if you will, of grant writing and the whole process of approaching foundations and other organizations for financial support. Many people find the foundation world bewildering or confusing or complicated; some even think it should be illegal, not that fraud is non-existent in this sector of American life. However, the process is rather straightforward, and there is the Foundation Center now known as "Candid" and its Foundation Directory to assist those seeking help navigating this world of financial assistance for churches, universities and colleges, charities and a myriad of organizations in the fields of social and environmental justice, education, housing and many other arenas of societal improvement.

Our first grant application was actually to the Presbyterian Church. Five members of The Presbyterian Committee for the Self-Development of People, each from a different locale across the nation, visited First AB Church of Harris Neck and spent more than two hours talking with Rev. Thorpe, other Board members and some of the Harris Neck elders and descendants. This site committee did the most thorough site visit I have ever seen. They left Harris Neck, seemingly satisfied they had what they needed to make a decision, and very soon Rev. Thorpe was notified we would soon be receiving our grant funds.

This was to be a one-time grant, as most grants are. Some foundations, especially larger ones, do award multi-year grants. It felt good to have funds in our treasury, and when Rev. Thorpe made the announcement at the next community meeting, people were indeed happy, though many were skeptical and most did not understand the process.

Other foundations would award us grants over the next few years, included the prestigious and social justice-focused Mary Reynolds Babcock Foundation, The Conservation Fund, Southern Partners Fund and the Nathan Cummings Foundation. Babcock would actually end up awarding us three grants. Most of the funds we received were for general operating expenses. I turned my home office into the Trust's office, complete with computer, phone, copier, fax, filing system and plenty of desk and wall space. It worked fine for our needs. The Board usually met at Rev. Thorpe's house, and we continued for years meeting first in the sacristy of FAB Church of Harris Neck, then in the church's Fellowship Hall, and much later in another space in Darien.

Chapter 8: Going to Washington

With the support of the McIntosh County Commissioners, we arranged our first meeting with U. S. Congressmen Jack Kingston (1st District) and John Barrow (12th District) of Georgia to inform them of the Movement and ask for their support. Both seemed interested in helping us. There were additional meetings with other Representatives and Senators, who we felt would be important to the eventual passage of legislation. Our meetings with Congressman Kingston and his staff became more frequent, with each meeting resulting in some additional work or research he or his staff asked us to do. No Congressman wants to be embarrassed or blindsided by information or occurrences about which they had been unaware.

At one of these meetings, Mr. Kingston expressed his strong desire to have U.S. Fish and Wildlife "on board" with the Trust before legislation was introduced. We started this effort at the refuge level but from the beginning we met with resistance. In late 2009, Congressman Kingston called Rev. Thorpe to inform him that he would host a meeting with FWS leadership and other key congressmen to discuss Harris Neck in greater detail and to see if everyone could find some common ground from which we could move forward.

On December 8, 2009, six key members of the Trust and County Commissioner Boyd Gault, who was recovering from recent hip surgery, boarded an Amtrak train in Savannah. The following morning we all walked to the Rayburn House Office Building for our meeting. The room filled up quickly with more than twenty people. Congressmen John Lewis and John Barrow attended as did the Chiefs of Staff for Congressmen John Conyers and James Clyburn. Fish and Wildlife was represented by Deputy Director Dan Ashe and SE Regional Director Cynthia Dohner, and their staffs.

After a fair amount of Harris Neck history was discussed and several questions were answered by the Trust, Mr. Kingston made a commitment to the Trust to seek an "equitable resolution" to this issue. He asked FWS and everyone in attendance to make the same commitment. Everyone did so. Near the conclusion of the meeting, Kingston again voiced his commitment and said he was not going to send the Trust representatives home with a false promise. He also said, for everyone's benefit, "We would not all be gathered here today if this were a white community." Kingston also impressed upon FWS the need to follow up this meeting with another early in the New Year. The meeting ended with congeniality in the air, everyone saying their warm good-byes. The six of us from Harris Neck remained afterwards to talk privately with Congressman Kingston.

The train ride back to Savannah was a joyous affair. We were all excited and those who had at first been mistrustful of Mr. Kingston said how happy they were with what he had said and how he had conducted the meeting. We were all hopeful. Rev. Thorpe and I sat together and talked about what we needed to do next and how to prepare for the next meeting with FWS, which we hoped would be arranged fairly soon.

The next meeting with FWS was called more quickly than I had expected. I was getting my first real taste of working with Congress and other higher-ups in the federal government, and I knew everything was going to take longer than anticipated, so I was pleased when FWS said they would host a meeting in March 2010. This meeting, however, would prove to be an exception; there would be long periods of time between most future meetings.

On March 10th, virtually the same group from Harris Neck, plus Dr. Otis Johnson, scholar and Savannah's second black mayor and a long-time friend of Harris Neck, attended the meeting held at FWS's Savannah offices in Hardeeville, South Carolina. Cynthia Dohner, the head of the Savannah Office, the agency's archaeologist and several other FWS staff were in attendance, as was Congressman Kingston's Chief of Staff, Chris Crawford.

Weeks earlier, Cynthia Dohner and I started planning the meeting together with a series of phone calls. She and I agreed to work together on a meeting agenda and to hire an independent facilitator, who FWS would pay. A week before the meeting, the facilitator that Ms. Dohner chose called Rev.Thorpe and me. Without knowing much about him, we agreed to his facilitating the meeting.

After introductions on the 10th, the group of more than fifteen sat around a large conference table. Copies of the meeting agenda were passed around the table. I noticed, immediately, this was not the agenda I had agreed to with Ms. Dohner. I brought this to the attention of Rev. Thorpe, sitting next to me. The meeting proceeded nonetheless.

It also became clear in how he conducted the meeting, and whom he called upon and how long he allowed them to speak, that the facilitator was not an independent person. More time was given to Ms. Dohner, and some of us from Harris Neck were cut off without finishing the points we were trying to make. The meeting ran for about two hours and many things were discussed. Those of us from Harris Neck were trying to find the common ground and the equitable resolution that all had agreed to in the meeting with Jack Kingston. When discussions turned to the people returning to the land to build some houses, Cynthia Dohner made it quite clear that the agency wouldn't permit any efforts that led to a transfer of title and the return of any land on Harris Neck to the people. The agency's archeologist, Rick Kanaski followed Dohner's strong comments with a reason of his own as to why the return of any land was impossible. He said that Harris Neck was "wall-to-wall" with cultural, Native American sites and no actions could be taken to disturb them.

The Harris Neck refuge had been set up mainly as a migratory bird refuge and agency efforts were directed specifically to the wood stork, which was on the Endangered Species List. At one point in our discussions that day, when Ms. Dohner was talking about the importance of this bird, Evelyn Greer, most eloquently, addressed Ms. Dohner and the whole gathering. She said she and everyone on Harris Neck grew up and lived with the wood stork, which she said they called by a different name, and that the entire community lived in complete harmony with all the birds and all the wildlife on Harris Neck. After another comment by Ms. Dohner in defense of the wood stork, Ms. Greer said, "You are saying the birds have more rights than the people." Ms. Dohner quickly responded, that was not what she meant, but it was indeed what she meant. The meeting ended not long afterwards.

Our hour-long ride home that day was not at all like the train trip three months earlier. It seemed that FWS was cutting off the path to legislation, which was the best way to obtain title to any or all of Harris Neck. I now realized I had been very naive about how this was all going to unfold, that FWS was going to do the right thing and cooperate with us and with Congressman Kingston.

The first thing I did the next day was look for an archeology firm in Georgia or South Carolina that might do a study of all the literature, regarding cultural sites on Harris Neck. It was well known that the entire coastal region was once home to different Indigenous people, such as the Creek, the Cherokee and the Guale but we needed to know what had been discovered on Harris Neck.

When I talked to several of those from Harris Neck, they each pushed back at this idea of possible cultural sites coming into conflict with our plans. They stated that they, the white landowners and Margret Ann Harris had been the only rightful, legal owners of the land of Harris Neck, and that the proof was in her Will and the War Department's 1945 map of the community. There was also the fact and that many people from Harris Neck, obviously, had Indian blood. Wilson Moran's own father was part Cherokee; his grandfather was the full-blooded Chief Red Feather. They were all correct; but I went looking for a firm that might be able to help us.

Quickly, I had a meeting set up with the archeology firm, Brockington & Associates outside of Atlanta. My meeting with John Brockington was not a long one. John was somewhat familiar with Harris Neck. He said he would do a review of all the relevant literature on Harris Neck and let us know what he found. Not two weeks later, I got a call from John, saying his report and a map were in the mail to me.

He had found a few sites on Harris Neck, which could mean as little as a fragment of a clay pot had been unearthed at some point in time, but he said a comprehensive cultural investigation of Harris Neck had, in fact, never been done. What he did say was that there were numerous sites found south of Harris Neck Road, and when his report arrived, the accompanying map did show scores of sites – all south of Harris Neck. John would not accept payment from the Trust.

I will not say that Mr. Kanaski's comment about the "wall-to-wall" cultural sites was an outright lie; I will give him the benefit of the doubt that he was simply mistaken. However, his comment was the first in a long line of statements by Ms. Dohner and other FWS staff that were completely false.

With each statement, as we did with Mr. Kanaski's, we did our due diligence and retained, sometime without charge, scientists or other professionals, who would disprove FWS claims. This, again, took time, but it was necessary, and it went directly to the advice Russ Marane had given Wilson and me at our first meeting: "You must eliminate every reason they can say no to you."

At the Trust's April meeting, it was decided that we would hold a press conference in June and that we would invite media reps from the coastal region from Jacksonville to Savannah. The church's leadership gave its approval to hold the press conference in the sacristy, something not normally done, and we prepared for the event the next month.

The church was mostly filled with Harris Neck elders and descendants, and the press was well represented. Wilson Moran gave an opening statement, and then he, Rev. Thorpe and Pastor Timmons answered questions. We had achieved our purpose. Several stories were run in newspapers and on the radio, and the story was out there again showing, that we would be in for a fight with Fish and Wildlife to get what was rightfully ours. We also started strategizing about a national media campaign.

Just a few weeks after our first press conference, Rev. Thorpe received a letter from FWS's Cynthia Dohner. In her letter, Ms. Dohner offered to explore the possibility of having an annual homecoming day for the people of Harris Neck and erecting a small informational kiosk about Harris Neck somewhere on the refuge. If this was her idea of an equitable solution, we realized how far apart we were in reaching any common ground. Rev. Thorpe felt the letter and the meaningless offer were so insulting that he chose not to reply.

The Board and I decided to go ahead full steam with a serious media campaign. I started pitching the story of Harris Neck, which I soon discovered pretty much sold itself, to the *Atlanta Journal Commerce, National Public Radio,* several TV networks and even the *New York Times.* The *Times* expressed interest from the beginning, but several more phone calls and the emailing of some key information and important documents were needed to sell them. After many calls, I offered their reporter, Shaila Dewan an exclusive on the story.

Ms. Dewan was soon in McIntosh County. She had done her research and was now meeting Wilson, Rev. Thorpe, Evelyn Greer, Mary Moran and many others. Her article, with a few color photos, was printed on the front page of the paper's Business Section on July 1, 2010. The publication of the story by the *Times* brought the media calling from all over the country. The *Times of London* even called and wrote a story the following week. We ended getting considerable print, radio and TV coverage.

Time went by, and the Trust and I continued working on one thing or another. More media attention followed. We met again with Congressman Kingston who told us he would work on getting our issue before Congress. More than a year later, Mr. Kingston called Rev. Thorpe to let him know that a congressional hearing on Harris Neck had been set for December 15, 2011.

I immediately contacted some of our Advisory Board members, especially Orson Porter and Kathleen Cleaver. Kathleen invited me to a party at her house in Atlanta, after which she and Natsu Saito, her attorney friend, presented me with the idea of doing a Mock Hearing to prepare those of us who would be testifying before Congress. Ms. Cleaver soon had the hearing set up at Emory University, and had asked several other law professors to play the parts of U. S. Representatives, who would be on the panel for the real thing.

Dan Biersdorf flew in from Minneapolis and many folks from Harris Neck drove the five hours to Atlanta to be part of the event, which was held in Emory's Law School. The mock hearing was exactly what we all needed to prepare for our actual day of testimony and Kathleen and Natsu's help proved invaluable.

On December 14th the Trust's leadership and I and several others from Harris Neck once again boarded an Amtrak train for DC. That night the five of us chosen to testify, sat up and talked through the parts we would each play the following day, and we did some role playing as to how to answer some hypothetical questions from the committee members.

The next morning, we all made our way to the Longworth House Office Building and the beautiful wood paneled chambers used by the House Committee on Natural Resources. After lots of excited greetings, the Oversight Hearing of the US House of Representatives Committee on Natural Resources, Subcommittee on Fisheries, Wildlife, Oceans and Insular Affairs was called to order by the Subcommittee Chairman John Fleming of Louisiana.

After Chairman Fleming's brief remarks and introductions, opening statements were made by the seven people facing the Subcommittee members some thirty feet away from their dais. Cynthia Dohner was the first to speak. She was followed by Dorothy Bambach representing, The Friends of the Savannah Coastal Wildlife Refuges. I was next to read my opening statement and was followed by Rev. Robert Thorpe, Wilson Moran, Winston Relaford and Evelyn Greer, who all talked about Harris

Neck from each of their unique perspectives.

Our preparation had paid off. We each did an excellent job with our own statements, all of which were entered into the Congressional Record, and we answered each committee member's questions completely and, I think, concisely. On the other hand, Ms. Dohner and Ms. Bambach seemed unprepared and I thought, somewhat arrogant in the way they responded to some of the questioning. Congressman Kingston was not a member of this Committee, but Chairman Fleming had invited him to join the panel. Mr. Kingston actually scolded Ms. Dohner for her many inadequate answers and her general lack of preparedness.

It was right after this hearing that I first met Harry Burroughs. When Mr. Kingston and all the members of the Trust, who had come to DC, were celebrating in the hallway outside the hearing's chamber, Harry walked up and introduced himself to Rev. Thorpe and me. Harry was the one who had put together the hearing, and he had spent his entire career on the Hill, as a Congressional aide in one capacity or another. I would much later find out that he was the main staffer on the National Wildlife Refuge System Improvement Act of 1995 that was written by Alaskan Representative Don Young.

Harry congratulated us on our testimony and made mention of his grandparents having lost their land via an eminent domain condemnation. From the first, Harry struck me as a smart, very knowledgeable and thoughtful man. At the end of our brief first meeting, he said to call him if we ever needed any help. We exchanged cards, and we were off to have dinner and catch our night train back to Savannah.

Once again, we had prepared and done our jobs well. It was not many weeks after our testimony that a letter from Chairman John Fleming arrived at the Trust's Post Office Box. I immediately telephoned Rev. Thorpe.

The train ride home was even more joyful than the one almost exactly two years earlier. The amount of time that had passed between the meeting in Jack Kingston's office and this Oversight Hearing, however, was not lost on Rev. Thorpe and me, but we were once again hopeful that with or without FWS's cooperation, which Congressman Kingston wanted, we would ultimately be successful – that legislation would pass and Harris Neck would be reclaimed.

On the train home, I talked with Rev. Thorpe about the idea of looking for a law firm that would represent the Trust from here forward, especially through the legislative process, which we knew would not be easy or fast. Rev. Thorpe's first response to my idea was that we could not afford to hire a law firm.

During the first movement, now thirty years past, attorney Clarence Martin, had represented Harris Neck's People Organized for Equal Rights. I was not there at the time, so I only know what Rev. Timmons and others told me about Mr. Martin's ability and, more importantly, the resources he may have had, and probably did not, at his disposal. In any event I thought we were now at a critical point in our journey and that we had done all the work we could do without good legal representation.

I certainly agreed with Rev. Thorpe that we did not have the money to hire a law firm, and getting a foundation to pay for legal counsel was not possible. However, the right law firm may take on our case pro bono. He said it was worth a try. So, I set out looking for a large firm. This search included talking with my attorney brother, Paul and with Orson Porter, our advisor in DC.

I had never heard of Rosewood, Florida and the massacre that occurred in the black community in 1923. A friend in New York said he had just watched a movie by the same name and suggested I should see it. I found the DVD and watched it that week. From the research I did following my viewing of this well-done movie, I discovered the horrific events portrayed in the film, which starred John Voight and Ving Rhames, were mostly true. I also read that the law firm that represented survivors and descendants of Rosewood, seventy years later, was Holland & Knight, one of

America's largest and most respected law firms.

Holland & Knight helped the Rosewood descendants receive a more than $2 million dollar settlement from the State of Florida and set up a college fund for Rosewood youth. The Governor of Florida also made a public apology to the Rosewood descendants, something unheard of, even in 1996.

So, I did some homework on Holland & Knight and found out that every one of its more than one thousand attorneys was required or, at least, strongly encouraged to provide a certain minimum number of hours of pro bono counsel every year. I called their Jacksonville, Florida office and was referred to their Atlanta office. A week after my call to Atlanta, I received a call from the assistant to Robert Highsmith, Executive Partner of the Atlanta office inviting us to a meeting in Atlanta.

The Trust's new Board Chair, William Collins and I drove to Atlanta. On March 12, 2012. Mr. Collins and Mr. Highsmith signed a Letter of Engagement between Holland & Knight and the Harris Neck Land Trust. The firm would represent the Trust, pro bono, in its efforts to reclaim Harris Neck. We now had the firepower we needed.

Later that same month, the important Gullah Geechee Cultural Corridor Heritage Commission, with which I had been keeping in touch, informed of the Trust's progress, passed a Resolution in support of the Harris Neck Land Trust and put the Resolution in its draft, Comprehensive Management Plan, which was then going through the public comment phase and would soon be published.

Emory Campbell, one of two commissioners from South Carolina on the Gullah Geechee Commission, and one of our Advisory Board members, called me to tell us that FWS representatives had called and pressured him to remove the Resolution from the Commissions Management Plan. Emory refused.

A few months later, at its summer conference in Savannah, the Georgia Association of Black Elected Officials

(GABEO) unanimously passed its own Resolution in full support of the Harris Neck Justice Movement. Many necessary elements were falling into place, but FWS still resisted a transfer of title of any land on Harris Neck. We kept the dialogue open.

Then in 2013, the Trust's leadership met with Congressman Kingston and Robert Highsmith at Holland & Knight's offices in Atlanta. Mr. Kingston had been talking with many Representatives on both sides of the aisle and with some US Senators, and he had come to the conclusion that a bill requesting any change of title on refuge land would not pass either the House or the Senate.

Confronted with this very discouraging news and with the growing dysfunction in Congress, the Trust reluctantly decided, with the counsel of Mr. Highsmith and Mr. Kingston, to pursue another route toward an equitable resolution. It was decided that a long-term, renewable lease of a smaller portion of Harris Neck would better suit the Trust's mission and objectives, given the realities of Congress. Holland &

Knight and the Trust went to work on the preparation of a lease.

On May 30, 2013 Cynthia Dohner and several members of FWS and the Department of Interior met with the Trust's leadership and Robert Highsmith in Atlanta. The Trust informed Dohner and the others of its concept of a lease of 700-800 acres of Harris Neck. FWS made no promises at this meeting, but it did seem that some headway was made with the talk of a lease, and they also like the idea of a Living Museum, which we mentioned.

I started looking for examples of such a lease in the entire Refuge system, and I called Harry Burroughs to get his ideas on this new route to resolution. Harry told me that such leases did exist in the system, and, in fact, there were companies that ran concession stands and provided fishing outings, tours, bicycling, kayaking and other tourist activities to refuge visitors across the country.

On August 27th the Trust hosted Cynthia Dohner and many of the FWS staff who had attended the meeting on

May 30th at Holland and Knight. This meeting, held in the Fellowship Hall of the Harris Neck church, was preceded by a dinner the night before at Jerome's Old School Diner, which is situated in the woods not far behind Wilson Moran's house. That dinner was a real treat for these out-of-towners, who had all commented on how fresh their shrimp or flounder or sea bass had been. It was a nice enough affair, but everyone from Harris Neck who attended later commented on how arrogant and heavy-handed Ms. Dohner and some of the others from FWS had been. This relationship was certainly not one of equals. She was playing her role as gatekeeper and supreme stonewaller very well.

On the morning of the 27th, Wilson Moran played tour guide in the large SUV in which Ms. Dohner arrived. Another FWS vehicle followed as we drove through the refuge before the tour was concluded at Barbour River Landing. As usual, Ms. Dohner did most of the talking, interrupting Wilson's tour repeatedly. She made not a single mention of the former community or the people of Harris Neck, but chose only to talk about the wood stork and all the other birds that the refuge was protecting.

Directly following the tour, we all met at the Fellowship Hall. With coffee mugs refreshed, everyone in the large gathering took their seats and Rev. Timmons called the meeting to order with a prayer. Dr. Otis Johnson also joined us. I sat between the former Mayor and Robert Highsmith. Ms. Dohner handed out the meeting agenda, to which I had contributed an item or two.

Ms. Dohner passed out a list of thirteen items she said the agency was willing to consider for Harris Neck. The only item that was of any interest to us was the last one – a Living Museum, plans for which we had already started.

Ms. Dohner clearly stated the agency's refusal to allow the construction of any houses, yet here they were talking about permitting the building of several structures of a living museum, such as a replica of an original homestead, a regular "static" museum, a replica of the Rosenwald Schoolhouse and other elements that would make such a museum interesting and sustainable.

She gave several reasons why houses would not be permitted on the refuge. She said Harris Neck was home to 357different species of birds including several pairs of the endangered Red Cockaded Woodpecker, and that human activity would be disruptive of their habitat. She said the wood stork, certainly could not tolerate such human activity that housing would bring. And finally, she said something that none of us had yet heard from her or anyone from FWS - that Harris Neck was a Maritime Forest and that because of the unique features of such a forest, and especially its "understory," housing could most definitely not be permitted.

I knew she was lying, and I felt my blood pressure rise with her arrogance. I was about to say something to her but Robert Highsmith noticed in time and gave me a light tap on my thigh. I refrained from speaking, and was later glad I had. It probably would not have gone so well.

Following the meeting, those from the Trust who remained, seemed deflated and complained about Dohner's arrogance and how ridiculous her "List of 13" was, except perhaps for the living museum. This museum, for me, however, seemed promising, and it seemed to be a good way for the Trust to get its foot in the door in Harris Neck. Who knew what may lay ahead with Congress? It was a start, and I decided to find something similar in the Refuge system that might be duplicated in our own fashion in Harris Neck and that might give people some real hope for better things in the future.

We continued working on different issues and tried to keep Harris Neck in public view. In early February 2014, we held a full-day Harris Neck Symposium at Savannah State University. The University sponsored the well-attended event that Dr. Johnson and three other professors were instrumental in arranging. The professors took the audience through the history of Harris Neck from Emancipation to the present, and then several of the elders sat up front and answered questions. It was a good event.

At the same time of my search of the refuge system for a living museum, I also found an ecologist, who we had to hire to refute Ms. Dohner's strong assertion that Harris Neck was a Maritime Forest, something everyone from Harris Neck already knew it was not. And I did more research on the wood stork and Red Cockaded Woodpecker. I found the correct number of bird species in Harris Neck (145), listed as such by the Audubon Society and Harris Neck's own annual Christmas Bird Count.

Every study on the wood stork by ornithologists that I read, with regard to the proximity of human activities to them and their nests, called for a 100-meter set-back. The plans we had for our living museum and accompanying elements would be more than 4,000 feet from Woody Pond, the main nesting site of the wood stork and egrets.

With regard to the Maritime Forest, the ecologist we hired was not long forwarding his report to us. It stated what we knew: Harris Neck was indeed not a Maritime Forest. It most likely had not been one since the days of the Guale

Indians, and perhaps much earlier than their habitation.

Once again, FWS had lied to us, or at best, had misrepresented the facts. I choose to believe Ms. Dohner simply lied, thinking that we were all a bunch of ignorant country folk, who did not know how to do some simple research, let alone carry out our ambitious plans for Harris Neck. These falsehoods and the on-going arrogance, and at times outright racism, to which the people of Harris Neck were subjected by FWS, made me more determined to find our way forward and never give up our goal.

With the help of Harry Burroughs, I found what I was looking for in the Great Basin Society, a non-profit environmental organization founded in 1971 on the immense Malheur National Wildlife Refuge in southeastern Oregon. I called and spoke to the Society's Executive Director and discovered that this organization had, for the past 40 years, been doing what we were now intending to do with a similar lease in Harris Neck.

Their lease was called a Cooperative Agreement, and the Director said she would be happy to send us a copy. When I told her of FWS's relentless stonewalling and resistance to the Trust, she said she did not understand why the FWS was treating us as they were, since her relationship with her FWS folks in Oregon was a good one. I asked myself was this because her membership and visitors were virtually all white and the people from Harris Neck were black?

In any event I found that the Great Basin Society had everything we had been considering for our living museum, and that they had, in fact, much more. They had several different types of lodging (a definite non-starter for the Trust), accommodating more than 120 visitors, a large dining room for as many guests, a static museum, a large activity/lecture hall, an RV park and much more. And plans were in the works for additional buildings.

In June of 2014, the Secretary of Interior, Sally Jewell visited Harris Neck to announce the removal of the wood stork from the Endangered Species List. It would now be listed as a threatened species. After her press conference, she agreed to meet with some of the Trust's leadership and Mary Moran, now 94. Advisors Al Williams and Dr. Otis Johnson also joined us. Since Secretary Jewell, who had been the CEO of REI, was not part of the entrenched bureaucracy in DC, we were hopeful she would help us.

She was quickly told the story of Harris Neck and its taking, and then Mrs. Moran, who sat near Ms. Jewell, talked about what that day in July 1942 was like. Her calm but passionate words seemed to reach Ms. Jewell; I think I even saw her eyes glisten. As the meeting ended, she asked us to include a Preliminary Site Plan with the lease application we told her we were preparing for submission to FWS.

As Ms. Jewell left Harris Neck in her motorcade, she passed dozens of people from Harris Neck, who had positioned themselves along Harris Neck Road, holding signs asking for justice and the return of the land.

A few months later, the Trust submitted a General Special Use Permit Application and a Preliminary Site Plan to the Department of Interior and US Fish and Wildlife. This application outlined our plans and requested a long-term, renewable lease to the eastern most portion of the Harris Neck Refuge, as far away from Woody Pond as was possible.

On February 26, 2015 the Trust's new Board Chair, Winston Relaford, Robert Highsmith and I met at the Department of Interior with Sally Jewell's Deputy Chief of Staff, Dan Ashe, now Director of Fish and Wildlife Service, his Deputy Director and an attorney from Interior to discuss our lease application and our site plan.

Our application was denied on the grounds that it was not an "Appropriate Use" of the land. However, FWS Director Dan Ashe then offered two possible paths forward toward an equitable resolution for the people of Harris Neck. The first was a land transfer, wherein the Trust would buy a piece of property that FWS deemed suitable as a bird habitat, and then the agency would exchange the same number of acres on Harris Neck with what the Trust had purchased.

Though the idea of a land transfer would be brought up many times over the next few years by FWS and though the Trust did consider it, Winston, Robert and I knew from the start that this was not a viable option. First of all, we did not have the money to buy any land. Depending on the number of acres we were talking about, we might have to raise $2 million or more.

Dan Ashe pointed out that we had a number of foundations supporting us and that perhaps they could combine their resources. Indeed, a couple of these foundations had expressed interest in helping us once we had reclaimed some land, but those would be funds to help us build our living museum. We would still have to raise a lot of money and we did not see any way to do this.

Secondly, it seemed appalling to me that the people of Harris Neck would have to buy their way back to their own land. And thirdly, I had heard that FWS talked a lot about land transfers but when it came down to it, these deals were rarely carried out successfully. And by now no one from Harris Neck trusted anything offered, or even said, by FWS.

The second option that Mr. Ashe mentioned, I liked, as did Winston Relaford and Robert Highsmith. Dan Ashe said that if, "You can prove the uniqueness of everything that has happened in Harris Neck since 1942, we will support legislation to return the land." We three were amazed at this offer, and again, it brought us back to looking at title and ownership of the land, not simply a lease, long-term or not.

Winston, Robert and I went to work on what we called the Uniqueness Document. It was not until May 2, 2016 that the three of us were back at the Department of Interior with Director Ashe and a smaller group than the previous meeting. With barely a word about why he denied us this opportunity, Dan Ashe turned our uniqueness document face down on his side of the table, and, once again, raised the idea of a land transfer.

The document we had labored over for months was an excellent piece of work, and the three of us thought it undoubtedly proved the uniqueness of Harris Neck. It listed all the elements, starting with the taking of the land in July 1942, that we thought proved the uniqueness of Harris Neck in the entire National Refuge System, but Dan Ashe disagreed.

Leaving the meeting that afternoon, Winston, Robert and I walked along Constitution Avenue and talked about how arrogantly Dan Ashe had closed this path forward on us. One of us said that any reasonable person would clearly see that we had proven uniqueness.
We were all very angry and deeply disappointed.

Donald Trump was now President and Robert Highsmith, a Republican, had friends in this new administration. It took some time to arrange our first meeting with some people he knew, but on July 31, 2017, Robert, Winston and I were sitting in a conference room in Holland & Knights DC offices being introduced to Billy Kirkland, Special Advisor to the

President and Steve Smith, Special Advisor to Ryan Zinke, the new Secretary of Interior.

Both of these men said they wanted to look at Harris Neck with fresh eyes and said they would look creatively for a way forward. They repeatedly said, "We are change agents." Steve Smith suggested we consider a Cooperative Agreement as a path toward resolution.

Though I was extremely doubtful that anything would come from the Trump administration that would be helpful to us, Winston and Robert were pleased with the meeting and, once again, seemed hopeful. In time, I too thought we just might get somewhere with the help of these two men, both of whom I liked and thought were sincere.

Because of Robert Highsmith's busy schedule and other delays, it wasn't until more than a year later that the Trust submitted a draft of a Cooperative Agreement similar to the one the Great Basin Society had with FWS. In this document the Trust asked for a 25-year, renewable lease of 500 acres in the eastern-most portion of the Harris Neck Refuge, more than 4,000 feet from Woody Pond, thereby assuring there would be absolutely no impact on the wood stork or any of the migratory bird species.

The actual number of acres that would be needed for the construction of our living museum and the accompanying buildings that would support the museum would be a fraction of that, not even 20 acres. Most of the land was to be kept as green space. We also wanted to build a few small cottages, not for the people of Harris Neck, but to be used as guest rentals for visitors to the refuge and to what the Trust was now calling the Harris Neck "Homeplace."

Several months later, the Trust approached Buddy Carter the new Congressman for Georgia's 1st District. Robert Highsmith knew Mr. Carter, another Republican. In August of 2019 Mr. Carter hosted a meeting in his Savannah office. Once again, the Trust's leadership and a junior attorney from Holland & Knight met with several FWS representatives. To the delight of those from the Trust, Cynthia Dohner was not in attendance. The word was she had retired or moved on to another position.

Winston Relaford and I had met several weeks earlier with Mr. Carter and his Chief of Staff. We brought copies of our draft Cooperative Agreement. When Mr. Carter realized that we were not seeking title to all or even part of Harris Neck but were requesting a lease to a small portion of the land, he seemed pleased. He was not in favor of our earlier position, but as he looked over our draft agreement, he said he would be glad to host a meeting of the parties and try to work out an equitable deal.

Early in the August meeting, the attorney from Holland & Knight commented on how long the Harris Neck people had been waiting for justice and how long we had been meeting with the Fish and Wildlife Service to find common ground. He smartly asked the FWS representatives if they would commit to finding an equitable solution to the Harris Neck issues within a matter of weeks or months, at most, and not allow this to drag out for yet another year or longer.

FWS made a commitment to this new timeframe.

Representative Carter hosted a second meeting two months later, and most of the people who attended the August meeting were once again present. We discussed our draft Cooperative Agreement again. We had brought maps and a drawing of The Homeplace to help with the discussion. FWS asked why we wanted 500 acres, which they thought was excessive. We explained that this land was sacred to the people of Harris Neck. It was where people were baptized and where some leaders of the former community had lived. We also said that 95 percent of our ask would be kept in green space. FWS wanted a much smaller number of acres.

That second meeting at Congressman Carter's ended with no plans for a next meeting and no real progress having been made, though FWS had committed to the weeks-to-months resolution timeframe. I put no trust in their commitment.

Then Covid hit. Nothing had come from the two Trump Administration special advisors, Billy Kirkland and Steve Smith, and it seemed we were now left in limbo. Nothing much happened for several months, while people everywhere started navigating life with the Coronavirus. Our regular in-person monthly community meetings came to a halt, but we soon picked them back up with Zoom meetings, and, surprisingly and happily, some new Harris Neck descendants were seen on our computer screens.

These new folks brought good energy to the meetings, and Winston and I and others in the Trust's leadership were once again encouraged. And then there was a new election and Joseph Biden became America's 46th President. And just as, or possibly more, important, Georgia had two new Senators, both Democrats.

Since Senator Rafael Warnock is from Savannah, I enquired of those in Harris Neck and those on our Advisory Board to see if anyone knew the Pastor, now Senator Warnock. Al Williams,

Kathleen Cleaver and Otis Johnson all said they had known Rev. Warnock for many years. They all spoke highly of him, each saying he was a good man and a man of his word.

With the help of Al Williams, we were soon speaking with Senator Warnock's Deputy Chief of Staff, Lawrence Bell. At the same time our community Zoom meetings took on a new, more assertive tone and spirit. At one of our first meetings after the election of Senators Warnock and Jon Ossoff, a couple of descendants raised the idea of pursuing title to a portion of Harris Neck, something we had given up on years ago.

They made a good case for returning to a quest for ownership, with our two new Georgia Senators, the composition of the new administration, and with President Biden's stated commitments to justice. There was also Biden's very important choice for the new Secretary of Interior, Native American Debra Haaland.

Over the next several months, Winston and I had several conversations with Mr. Bell. We sent him the War Department's 1945 map and many other documents we thought would educate him about Harris Neck so he could intelligently inform and advise t the Senator. Al Williams had told us that Mr. Warnock knew about Harris Neck, but neither Winston nor I were sure of how much he knew. We tried not to miss anything that would be important to Lawrence Bell or the Senator.

After months of discussions and many of our requests of Lawrence Bell to visit Harris Neck, he finally said he would be able to come on September 3, 2021. He and three others from Sen. Warnock's Atlanta and Savannah offices arrived early on the 3rd. With a very short notice, Robert Highsmith even flew in on a friend's small plane, landing at the single Eagle Neck airstrip a few miles west of Harris Neck.

Al Williams also joined several Harris Neck descendants for most of that warm summer day. After introductions, Wilson Moran took Lawrence Bell and the other Warnock representatives on a tour of Harris Neck.

That was followed by a boat ride in the estuary and then a long luncheon in the screened gazebo in front of Jerome's Old School Diner.

I was not there that day, but I heard from Winston and others that with this visit Lawrence seemed to understand what had happened at Harris Neck and to its people at a much deeper and more profound level. This is exactly what we had all been hoping for, and it is the reason why we had tried so hard to get him to visit. There is no substitute for walking the land of Harris Neck and going out on the water.

We all hoped Lawrence would go back to DC with a passion to do the right thing and report favorably to the Senator. Though it again took some time, we finally met, via Zoom, on December 15, 2021 with Senator Warnock. Lawrence Bell and three of us from Harris Neck were on the phone. Otis Johnson and Al Williams were also able to join us.

The Senator expressed his appreciation for what we had been doing over all these years with the Harris

Neck movement and said he was passionate about Harris Neck and was committed to helping us. We made it clear that we were, once again, pursuing title to 500 acres of Harris Neck, and that the Refuge itself would not be affected in any way.

We pointed out that the acreage we are seeking is on the eastern side of the Refuge, and that Refuge visitors don't even see this area, unless they were to get out of their cars and walk the narrow path into this densely wooded section. The one-way road that meanders through the refuge is west of the acreage we are requesting.

We did not speak much about the two avenues to our hoped-for ownership – legislation or a Presidential Executive Order – but the meeting went well and all of us from Harris Neck were, once again, hopeful. After the call, I phoned Dr. Johnson to thank him for joining us and expressed my disappointment that the call had not lasted longer and that we had not gotten down to the details of how the Senator might want to proceed. Dr. Johnson chuckled and said, "Dave, you just had a thirty-minute meeting with a US Senator. That's a big deal."

Subsequent to the December meeting, Robert Highsmith put together a draft piece of legislation and sent it to Senator Warnock. Lawrence Bell told us that the Senator planned on meeting with Interior Secretary Haaland, as the first step in clearing the way for either the introduction of legislation or an Executive Order, which would be faster, cleaner and simpler.

July 27, 2022 marked the 80th anniversary of the official taking and condemnation of Harris Neck. The people have waited and fought a very long time for justice. This movement is now in its 17th year, and the people, who are still active with the Harris Neck Land Trust, remain hopeful that the right thing will finally be done.

Chapter 9: Still Searching

In the fall of 2011, I removed from my in-box a letter written by Congressman Jack Kingston of Savannah, Georgia. The letter was addressed to the Chairman of the House Natural Resources Committee, Doc Hastings of Pasco, Washington. The purpose of the correspondence was a request that the Subcommittee on Fisheries, Wildlife, Oceans and Insular Affairs conduct an oversight hearing on the Harris Neck National Wildlife Refuge.

In the 20 years, I served as the Republican Subcommittee Staff Director, I reviewed dozens of similar request letters from Democrat and Republican members. It was my job to select the topics for a potential hearing and obtain the approval of my Subcommittee Chairman. Prior to my discussion with Subcommittee Chairman John Fleming, I undertook a comprehensive investigation of Harris Neck, Georgia.

While I had passed the exit for Harris Neck on I-95 many times on my way to Florida, I had not visited the refuge nor did I know about the community of Harris Neck. I wanted to find out about the history of the Harris Neck National Wildlife Refuge. For instance, when was it established, under what legal authority, what were its missions, how was the land acquired and who were the previous property owners? What I learned was disconcerting.

I was shocked to find out that the previous property owners were the descendants of former slaves. It was also apparent that black landowners did not receive the same level of compensation as their former white neighbors. In the legal profession, a lawyer will frequently ask whether a claim or assertion can "Pass the Smell Test." In the case of the Harris Neck Refuge, how the land was acquired and how its former owners were treated smelled like an injustice.

With this information, I met with Chairman Fleming and strongly recommended an oversight hearing. Without hesitation, he agreed and directed me to contact Congressman Kingston's office to ascertain which witnesses they would like to invite to the hearing. One week later, we issued a public notice announcing that the oversight hearing would be held on December 15, 2011. As the majority party, we invited Jack Kingston, Congressman of Georgia's 1st District, the U.S. Fish and Wildlife Service and representatives of the Harris Neck Land Trust. The Democrats invited Dorothy Bambach, the Conservation Chair for the Friends of the Savannah Coastal Wildlife Refuges.

At 10:00 a.m. on Wednesday, December 15, 2011, Chairman John C. Fleming convened the hearing. I had the great pleasure of working with Chairman Fleming for four years. John Calvin Fleming, Jr. is a compassionate, kind and remarkable man. He was born in Meridian, Mississippi and obtained both an undergraduate and medical degree from the University of Mississippi.

After graduation, he served in the United States Navy with the highest distinction. Among his assignments were the Chief Resident of the Family Practice at the Naval Regional Medical Center at Camp Pendleton, family medicine on the

Island of Guam and Director of the Navy's Drug and Alcohol Treatment Program.

After leaving the Navy, he established a medical practice in Minden, Louisiana in 1982. Dr. Fleming was named Louisiana Family Practice Physician of the Year in 2007. In addition, he acquired 36 Subway Sandwich Shops and UPS stores in 182 outlets in Louisiana, Mississippi and Texas. These stores provide well paying jobs to hundreds of hard working men and women. In 2008, Dr. John Fleming became a Member of Congress representing Louisiana's 4th Congressional District. He defeated his Democratic opponent, Paul Carmouche by 350 votes out of nearly 93,000 cast.

One of his first acts as a Member of Congress was to invite a constituent to witness the historic inauguration of Barack Obama as our 44th President. This person sat with Dr. Fleming on the raised dais on the West Front of the U.S. Capitol. Dr. Fleming chose as his special guest, revered Civil Rights icon Mamie Love Wallace. She met Dr. Martin Luther King, Jr. in Shreveport, Louisiana in 1959, and with his support and encouragement, the North Louisiana Civil Rights Movement was born.

In his opening statement on December 15, 2011, Chairman Fleming opined, "The residents who lived on Harris Neck were given two weeks to move themselves and all of their belongings. They were allegedly told that they could reclaim their property at the end of World War II and that they would be fairly compensated. Sadly, it appears that neither of these promises were ever kept."

In his opening remarks, the ranking Democrat member of the Subcommittee, Gregorio Kilili Cammacho Sablan of Saipan in the Northern Marina Islands said, "Today, we will hear testimony from witnesses regarding the history of Harris Neck National Wildlife Refuge. I look forward to learning more about this important issue."

The first witness was Congressman Jack Kingston. He testified, "This is the first hearing that the Harris Neck residents have ever been able to have, and yet this is a situation that has been going on really for decades. And it is a question to me of, what was the original intent of the U.S. Government, was there compensation that was fair to the residents, and was the original intent followed in terms of reverting the land back to the residents of it?"

Jack Kingston can be forgiven for not knowing about the first Harris Neck hearing 32 years earlier. He was a young man living in Savannah, Congressman Bo Ginn had died in 2005 and there were only a few members of Congress left from the 96th Congress. He deserves great credit for requesting the hearing and giving his constituents the opportunity to persuade the Committee that they should restore this land to its rightful owners.

The second witness was Cynthia Dohner, the Southeast Regional Director, of the U.S. Fish and Wildlife Service. Her office was located in Atlanta, Georgia and Harris Neck NWR was one of the 131 national wildlife refuges managed by this region. In her testimony, Director Dohner said, "The condemnation of private property sometimes presents difficult issues, especially in time of war. Some may see these situations and decisions as unfair. However, it does not mean that people were not fairly compensated, or that laws and regulations were not followed appropriately. The Service is not aware of any unfair treatment or unlawful activity related to this condemnation."

This is a remarkable statement. It is true the Fish and Wildlife Service did not condemn the Harris Neck property, communicate with the landowners or decide to compensate only for the "fair market" value of the land. Nevertheless, in the second paragraph of Director Dohner's oral testimony, she stated, "The Service is not in possession of the original records pertaining to DOD's condemnation of these lands." So, if the Service did not have these vital records and had not seen them, how can Cynthia Dohner categorically state that there was no unfair treatment or unlawful activity?

In its 1985 Report to Congress, the United States General Accounting Office concluded, "As a result of the absence of land and property tax assessment records, we were unable to evaluate the acquisition payments to the former Harris Neck landowners for their land and whether there was racial discrimination in determining the compensation."

The third witness was Dorothy Bambach, representing the Friends of the Savannah Coastal Wildlife Refuges. This group enjoys the tax benefits of being a 501(c)(3) charitable organization that can receive tax-deductible donations. Under federal law, this Friends Group is prohibited from engaging in any political activity and lobbying "except to an insubstantial degree." The Friends of the Savannah Coastal Wildlife Refuges was established in 2007. It is headquartered in Savannah, Georgia.

In her statement, Ms. Bambach said, "My experience as a volunteer has allowed me to see firsthand what a valuable and enduring asset Harris Neck is to the local government and the nation. And I empathize greatly with the families of the Harris Neck Land Trust for the sacrifices they made during this country's World War II efforts. But I strongly support the refuge, and I do not want to see it diminished by converting any part of it to residential or commercial use."

She also repeated the fallacious argument that, "While she (Margret Harris) did will her property to Mr. Delegall, none of those properties are within the Refuge boundary." This statement is pure nonsense. And, even if some of Margret Harris' lands were not condemned in 1942, in the words of Hillary Clinton "What difference does that make." There is no one who has ever questioned that the residents of Harris Neck legally owned the property that was taken from them by the federal government. The proof is right there in the War Department's 1945 map of Harris Neck.

She ended her testimony with, "Losing Harris Neck National Wildlife Refuge to development would be an economic, cultural and environmental tragedy. We ask the Subcommittee to ensure that the refuge remains intact, undisturbed, and under the leadership and control of the U.S. Fish and Wildlife." In short, this Friends Group doesn't care if the Harris Neck community was treated unfairly or if they were the victims of a monumental tragedy by the federal government. Sadly, they have shown no interest in ending this injustice.

During my 20 years working on the House Natural Resources Committee, I heard testimony from various Friends Groups. I can't recall a single time when they weren't in lockstep with the U.S. Fish and Wildlife Service. There are more than 200 Friends Groups throughout the United States, which tirelessly advocate on the agency's behalf.

In the case of the Friends of the Savannah Coastal Refuges, on their website, you can click on the "Harris Neck Land Issue." What you will find are links for the Fish and Wildlife Service's Harris Neck NWR, FWS summary of the issue and the agency's "Fact Sheet" on Harris Neck. What is interesting is that according to their publicly filed federal tax form 990, the Friends of Savannah donated over a two-year period $179,989 to the U.S. Fish and Wildlife Service's Savannah Coastal Refuges Complex located in Hardeeville, South Carolina. This was an enormous amount of money and it leaves little doubt that this Friends Group has a vested interest in maintaining the status quo in the seven refuges including Harris Neck that are managed by this complex.

On October 30, 2013, Regional Director Cynthia Dohner presented Dorothy Bambach with an award for her volunteer service to the refuge system. Let me be clear. I am not disparaging either Dorothy Bambach or the Friends of the Savannah Coastal Wildlife Refuges. They are entitled to their own opinions. They are not entitled, however, to their own facts and many of their assertions are simply wrong. They are convinced the Fish and Wildlife Service must keep this property at all costs and it is, therefore, not surprising they have consistently parroted the positions of the agency.

Apparently, this Friends Group was unaware of the Mike Wallace interview with FWS Savannah Project Leader John Porter Davis in 1983. Mike Wallace asked him, "If (Harris Neck Refuge) this were to disappear from the face of the earth, this 2,687 acres, the republic would not be subverted and the bird and deer population would not die from trauma.

Would they? John Davis' response was, "Probably not in all reality."

The last five witnesses were representatives of the Harris Neck Land Trust. David Kelly the Project Coordinator started the discussion. In his comprehensive testimony, he presented a number of important facts. These included:

(1). The original taking via eminent domain was highly illegal.

(2). The taking of Harris Neck was not just, not by a long measure, because first, not everyone was paid. Some people still have their deeds.

(3). Not a single African American family was paid for anything but their property. There were no payments for any improvements.

(4). Payments from the Federal Government did not go directly to the African American families and not in time, as required by the statute.

In closing, Mr. Kelly told the Subcommittee members that, "After the war the government did not talk with the original owners, did not contact them, and the land went to the county. It does not matter how Fish and Wildlife came to control Harris Neck. What matters is that the original taking was illegal, and therefore, each transfer of title since, according to our attorney, is invalid."

Board Member Wilson W. Moran, who is a direct descendant of Robert Delegall, told the members, "The War Department needed a place in which to build an airbase. Our white county leaders steered them to the community of Harris Neck. Our government claimed eminent domain, giving us two weeks to move out. In the blink of an eye, we were wiped out. We lost everything including our culture. Now we are all back to zero again."

Reverend Robert H. Thorpe, Pastor of the Peaceful Zion Church, testified, "Mr. Banks came to our house, and my grandfather went out and spoke with him and I went along. Mr. Banks said he represented the Federal Government and that the government needed our property for an army airbase. Then my grandfather asked him, 'If you take our property, are we going to get it back.' And Mr. Banks said, 'Yes, when the government is finished with it they will return it back to you."

Reverend Thorpe was 11-years-old when this conversation occurred. Like most Harris Neck residents, he worked on the family farm. This required toiling all spring, summer and fall in the hot oppressive fields of South Georgia, trying to scrape out an existence with fruit trees and subsistence crops. When they were ordered to leave Harris Neck in July 1942, it was the beginning of the harvest season. In his testimony, Reverend Thorpe told the members, "At the time our crops were just maturing and we had to leave all that behind us and that was part of our living. Corn, potatoes, beans, tomatoes, all our fruit and nut trees. All that was left behind was destroyed."

Why was the federal government so cruel to deny these farmers the fruits of their labors? Why couldn't these crops be harvested rather than destroyed? Why couldn't the federal government compensate them for their crop losses? Sadly, the simple answer is that the federal government had the power, and they didn't really care what happened to poor black farmers.

The fourth witness was Evelyn Greer. She had testified in 1979 and was now 84-years-old. Her compelling message was, "We are here today not as beggars. We are here to see and ask you all to let justice prevail. We need the property. God made arrangements for the birds and the bees, but he said the Son of Man has no place to lay his head. My home was burned, and everything I saw. There was no place to go."

The final witness was the Vice Chair of the Harris Neck Land Trust, Winston B. Relaford, Sr. In his testimony, he stated, "What was done to the Harris Neck Community in 1942 was an injustice, a wrong that must be righted. And this Committee has within its power to move on behalf of a neglected portion of America's citizenry. Let history show that you stood up today and began the process of making right an awful wrong."

With all the testimony presented, the Subcommittee members began the question-and answer portion of the hearing. Dr. Fleming repeatedly asked FWS Regional Director Cynthia Dohner, "Does the Service believe a remedy is required?" On his seventh attempt, Director Dohner responded, "I believe that the Service can offer additional things to the community, things like a National Heritage Day, but the Service doesn't have the authority to administratively give these lands back."

What she was referencing to was Public Law 94-579. This statute prohibits the Secretary of the Interior from modifying or revoking any withdrawal that added lands to the National Wildlife Refuge System. However, there are exceptions. The Fish and Wildlife Service can dispose of refuge lands if: the disposal is part of an authorized land exchange, cooperative agreement with a state or local government or if the Secretary determines the lands are no longer needed for the refuge system and the Migratory Bird Conservation Commission approved the disposal. I am not aware of a single instance when the Fish and

Wildlife Service has disposed of refuge lands because they were no longer needed for the system. This simply doesn't happen.

The Ranking Democrat, Gregorio Sablan first asked Dorothy Bambach, "Would you please provide us some example of how volunteers such as yourself, support the Harris Neck National Wildlife Refuge, please?" His second and final question was to Director Dohner. He asked her, "Would you please describe how the Service affects your efforts to support the tens of thousands of visitors who come to the Harris Neck National Wildlife Refuge each year?" There were no questions of the Harris Neck Land Trust Panel and I found that odd. I had always found Congressman Sablan, who is the first delegate elected from the Northern Marinas, to be engaging and inquisitive. In this case, both he and the Democratic staff were not engaged and were anxious for this hearing to be over.

Congresswoman Colleen Hanabusa of Hawaii reminded the Subcommittee that, "During the same timeframe,

Japanese Americans were relocated. And there is a U.S. Supreme Court case that said there was nothing wrong with that, as well. So simply because the courts may say there is nothing wrong with it, it doesn't necessarily then say that the injustice that was committed is somehow right."

She then asked a number of probing questions of Director Dohner. For instance, she asked, "Is there anything in writing of the results of the legal reviews that you have done? The answer was: "We do have some of that information, yes." "Can you also provide us with that" Answer was "Yes." No additional information was ever provided to the Subcommittee by the U.S. Fish and Wildlife Service.

Congressman Jack Kingston was then given an opportunity to question the witnesses. He asked Director Dohner, "Here is the compensation answer. Do you know why Fish and Wildlife has not given the information to the Committee yet? Her response was: "No sir, I don't. But trust me, you will get it very soon." It is now 11 years later. Cynthia Dohner is no longer Regional Director, John Fleming and Jack Kingston are no longer Members of Congress and the Fish and Wildlife Service never sent any follow-up information. Sadly, this is a dodge performed by federal agencies every day. They promise to send the information requested for the official record and in far too many cases they never do.

Congressman Kingston then posed several questions to Dorothy Bambach. His first inquiry was: "Ms. Bambach, you are not from that area? You moved in 1999? Her response was, "That is correct." In fact, she moved to Savannah in 1999. She never lived, went to school, worked or paid taxes to McIntosh County, Georgia.

He then told her, "Ms. Bambach, the reason why this is an important issue to us in Congress - and I want also you and the Friends organization to know, this is the political equivalent of me walking in a gasoline factory smoking a cigarette. It is a lose-lose in terms of the politics of this stuff. I understand two highly energized groups are in conflict here. But, as Americans, we can be united on the central question of fair compensation. And if the compensation was fair at that time, that is what we need to know. And people might not like that answer, one side or the other, but, to me, that is the empirical question."

Congressman Kingston closed his remarks by saying, "This is a case of two enormously important values: Justice being number one, and then you have the Gullah Geechee Corridor. It is my hope that we can stay engaged and try to come up with what really did happen in the 1940's and then where do we go from there."

At the conclusion of the hearing, Dr. Fleming submitted for the hearing record several documents. These included the Resolution adopted by the McIntosh County Board of Commissioners in 2007 stating, "The Board of Commissioners hereby recognizes the Harris Neck Land Trust and encourages and supports the Trust with its efforts to regain these 2,688 acres of Harris Neck from the Federal Government."

There are two primary reasons why the McIntosh County Board of Commissioners has strongly supported the Harris Neck Land Trust for the past 15 years. First, they believe an injustice has occurred and the federal government has a sacred obligation to return all, or some, of the 2,688 acres to the descendants of the former property owners. Second, these elected representatives understand that the establishment of the Blackbeard Island NWR, Harris Neck NWR and Wolf Island NWR have been an economic drain on the county. These 13,568 acres cannot be taxed by McIntosh County.

In 1935, Congress enacted the Refuge Revenue Sharing Act. The purpose of this law is to compensate local communities for lost tax revenues. According to the McIntosh County Tax Commissioners Office, they collected in 2022, $565.75 in property taxes for every home assessed at $50,000. Hypothetically, if 100 families were allowed to own a dwelling on Blackbeard Island, Harris Neck and Wolf Island, they would pay $56,575 in property taxes. This is a conservative figure. There were 84 property owners in Harris Neck in 1942.

If you increase the price for the same 100 homes to $100,000, then the county would receive $111,350. This is based on the current county tax rate of $1,113.50 for each dwelling. In reality, McIntosh County received $5,628 in refuge revenue sharing payments from the federal government. This means the county lost between $50,947 and $105,722 in tax revenues.

To make matters worse, the federal government is only paying 21 percent of what the county is entitled under this law. What the county should be getting is about $28,000 in refuge revenue sharing payments each year. The last time any county obtained full compensation was in 1975. Funding for this program has not been a priority of either the Fish and Wildlife Service or the United States Congress for almost 50 years.

For the past 40 years, I have repeatedly heard that national wildlife refuges are economic engines for local communities. While this is true for the Chincoteague National Wildlife Refuge in Virginia, Ding Darling National Wildlife Refuge in Florida and the Okefenokee

National Wildlife Refuge in Georgia, the vast majority of refuges, enjoy only a small, if any, economic benefit.

I have visited Chincoteague, Ding Darling and Okenfenokee. What they have in common is that within each refuge there are private companies known as concessionaires that offer various services to the visiting public. These include things like bicycle, canoe and kayak rentals, boat tours, educational programs, fishing guides, food services, gift and nature stores, pontoon boats, sunset rookery paddle tours and tram tours of wildlife.

Those who take advantage of these amenities contribute to the local economies. In the case of the three national wildlife refuges in McIntosh County, the only private companies who make money are those involved in transporting visitors to the Blackbeard Island National Wildlife Refuge. According to a representative of the Coastal Adventures of Georgia company, they would transport two people to Blackbeard Island from Shellman Bluff for a three-hour stay for $300 dollars. Harris

Neck has no concessionaries and Wolf Island National Wildlife Refuge is closed to the public.

On July 10, 2019, the U.S. Fish and Wildlife Service released its latest update on the economic contributions of national wildlife refuge visitation on local communities. In this *Banking on Nature Report*, the agency, analyzed 162 of the 567 national wildlife refuge units. FWS estimated that in 2017, 53.6 million visitors generated $3.2 billion of economic output in local communities.

The top three refuges were: Oregon Islands NWR with 10.2 million visitors creating $665,081 in economic activity; Chincoteague NWR with 6.9 million visitors generating $390,817 and Wichita Mountains NWR with 4.4 million visitors producing $98,000 in economic activity.

In Georgia, the report included Okefenokee and Savannah National Wildlife Refuges. In 2017, 723,508 visitors explored some of the 402,000 acres of the Okenfenokee NWR. They spent $64,700 affecting three counties in Georgia and one in Florida. During this same period, 391,439 people enjoyed the 31,551 acres of the Savannah NWR located within three counties in Georgia and South Carolina. Their economic contribution was $8,849 or $2,949 per county. None of the three refuges in McIntosh County were mentioned in the report. Nevertheless, it is clear that none of these visitations begin to offset the lost tax revenues to their respective local communities.

The Subcommittee also received a number of letters in support of the Harris Neck Land Trust. Dr. Otis S. Johnson, Mayor of Savannah, Georgia wrote, "This is a situation that has cried out for justice for almost 70 years. I have supported the efforts of the Harris Neck Land Trust over the years as they have waged a gallant struggle to regain land that was taken from them to support the World War II effort."

Georgia State Representative Al Williams opined, "The 75 families who owned this land from 1865-1942 were given three weeks to move off their land. Their crops, houses and other buildings were bulldozed and burned. Although there was small compensation given, they were promised that at the end of World War II the land would be returned. Indeed, it was deeded to McIntosh, Georgia."

The Gullah Geechee Cultural Heritage Corridor Commission submitted a Resolution that stipulated, "Support for the Harris Neck Land Trust and the Harris Neck Justice Movement in their efforts to reclaim the 2,687 acres of Harris Neck taken wrongfully, illegally and unjustly by the federal government, and return this land to its rightful owners."

Tyrone Banks, President of the Georgia Association of Black Elected Officials wrote, "GABEO stands with the Harris Neck Justice Movement in their effort to reclaim the 2,687 acres of Harris Neck land taken by the federal government in 1942."

Norman G. Kurland, President of the Center for Economic and Social Justice told the Subcommittee, "The Harris Neck community, as it existed up until 1942, they were a people who had created a strong, spiritual order where the ethic of personal responsibility yielded a communal self-sufficiency. They were a people who endured the horrors of slavery and then built a thriving community by their own hard work, ingenuity and commitment to each other, and they were living the American dream until our government destroyed their way of life in the summer of '42."

Finally, Director Edward J. Pennick of the Federation of Southern Cooperatives Land Assistance Fund wrote, "We believe that a great injustice was done to this community and its citizens - an injustice that has been felt for generations. We truly hope that you will take this opportunity to address this injustice by supporting the land use plan developed by the Harris Neck Land Trust, a plan that we believe serves the best interests of all parties."

On May 16, 2012, the President of the non-profit Friends of the Savannah Coastal Wildlife Refuges, Richard O. Shields wrote to Congressman Jack Kingston. In his letter, he stated that, "We also share the concern that you and all Americans have with regard to racial justice and equitable treatment of all citizens by our government." Clearly, his organization doesn't believe that equitable treatment should be extended to the Harris Neck Land Trust. Over the years in various meetings, they have expressed no willingness to give up even an inch of the Harris Neck National Wildlife Refuge.

Shields then added, "It is important that actions be based on facts." He is absolutely correct. Once again, here are the facts: black landowners received far less compensation than those white or racial unidentified property owners; in 1962 the agricultural lands were improperly reclassified to deny their return to black and white property owners; the condemnation process was fatally flawed and promises made to the former Harris Neck residents were ignored. Even Sheriff Tom Poppell admitted, "They were told that they would get their property back after the war."

Finally, he regurgitated the FWS's position that, "Consider the consequences of returning all or part of this refuge to descendants of those who owned less than half of the land purchased by the Department of Defense to create Harris Neck Army Airfield: no government-owned land in this country will be safe from similar claims."

I suspect the writer was unaware that the Harris Neck Land Trust represents both descendants of black and white former landowners. The Trust is not seeking a return of the entire refuge. The assertion that Harris Neck will open the floodgates is ludicrous. I have worked on refuge issues for over 40 years; Harris Neck is the only one created on land owned by former slaves. Since the first Congressional hearing in 1979, no additional claims of any group of descendants of former slaves have been filed. However, if such a group comes forward in the future, isn't it the responsibility of the federal government to correct injustices wherever they occur?

More than a year before this day of Congressional testimony, when Cynthia Dohner and many other FWS staff were preparing for a meeting with the Harris Neck Land Trust leadership, an FWS employee, who was involved in the preparations for that March 2010 meeting, told Dave Kelly, "This (FWS's opposition) is not about the wood stork or any of the birds or wildlife there, this is all about the Service not giving up a single acre in its entire system. That's what this is about."

Regrettably, the lobbying efforts of the Friends of the Savannah Coastal Wildlife Refuges were successful. In the September 6, 2012 edition of *The Brunswick News,* Tim Wessinger, a spokesman for Congressman Jack Kingston said, "The Congressman's role has probably ended in the dispute. Jack isn't taking a side one way or another. He's the facilitator to both sides. The Department of Interior will make a decision."

Interior's decision has been consistently to do absolutely nothing to address these legitimate claims. What is deeply troubling is that for a number of years the Fish and Wildlife Service hasn't utilized eminent domain and when it has, it has always fully compensated property owners for both the land and any improvements. This had been the case during my nearly four-decade career on Capitol Hill.

I can say with some certainty that if Jack Kingston had introduced and worked for legislation similar to those sponsored by Congressman Bo Ginn, the House Natural Resources Committee would have favorably reported the measure to the House of Representatives. I like to think the Speaker of the House, John Boehner would have allowed consideration of this important bill in the People's House.

Did the Trust's leadership make a misjudgment when it took Congressman Kingston's advice in 2012 – when he told the Trust he did not think a bill would ever get through the House – and changed the goal from seeking title to the land to seeking some sort of lease? Sadly, we will never know the answer to this question and the fight for justice marches forward.

Chapter 10: Going Back Home

On May 13, 1865, the last battle of the American Civil War was fought at the Palmito Ranch near Brownsville, Texas. Colonel Theodore H. Barrett of Orangeville, New York, commanded the Union forces. The largest contingent of his troops were members of the 62nd U.S. Colored Infantry Regime. Despite both sides knowing that Robert E. Lee had surrendered, these African American troops fought valiantly for their freedom.

This was the end of this four-year bloody conflict that cost the lives of 620,000 Union and Confederate troops including 40,000 black soldiers. The economy of the south was destroyed. Slavery was dead and cotton was no longer king. Hundreds of plantations were abandoned, damaged or burned to the ground. From this devastation, the bells of freedom rang loudly for the 4 million Americans who had been enslaved.

Slavery is the worst thing that ever happened in the United States. The institution was an abomination. It was evil, inhumane and rotten to the core. No human being ever wants to be held against their will. I have often wondered what would have happened to slavery, if the slave owners were forced to labor for 16 to 18 hours a day in their own cotton or rice fields. I suspect this horrible institution would have died long before 1865. For the vast majority of the Post Civil War emancipated people, they faced an uncertain future and terrible hardships because real freedom is economic freedom.

Out of the ashes of the Civil War, one Georgia plantation owner, Margret Ann Harris emerged and did something truly remarkable. Her white overseers had cheated her. Instead of trusting another charlatan, she appointed an ex-slave, Robert Delegall as her overseer and she placed in his hands her future and that of her son, Bright. She enshrined this arrangement in her "Last Will and Testament" signed on September 2, 1865 on Saint Catherine's Island, Georgia.

In the 157 years since she signed this document, no one has ever challenged its provisions or legality. It said simply: "Assign forever to have and to hold possess and convey all rights and titles --- of land lying and being in the County of McIntosh State of Georgia." For the next 77 years, about 70 African American families lived on the 2,867 acres known as Harris Neck.

These were poor, hard-working folks who never complained or asked for a government handout. They built a thriving, self-sufficient community with their Gullah Geechee culture, authentic food, Christian faith and strong work ethic. Within their community, they had their own businesses, cemeteries, churches, farms, homes, a school house and even a United States Post Office.

They lived quietly in an isolated community and compared to their ancestors, it was an idyllic existence. They simply wanted to be left alone, to live their lives and raise their children.

In 1942, their community and their way of life literally came to an end. The powerful federal government could have chosen to build its Army Airbase on many other suitable, uninhabited areas in McIntosh County. Instead, like locust or some other pestilence, it descended on Harris Neck. Our government burned their crops, homes and businesses. Why did this happen? The answer is racism. This should never have occurred and Harris Neck should never have become a national wildlife refuge.

Over the years, the federal government has made some monumental mistakes. Three of the worst were the internment of 120,000 Japanese Americans, the unlawful taking of 15,000 acres from the Colorado Indian Tributes and the destruction of Harris Neck community.

On August 10, 1988, President Ronald W. Reagan signed the Civil Liberties Act (P.L. 100-383) into law. This long overdue federal legislation included a formal Presidential apology to every surviving U.S. citizen or legal immigrant of Japanese ancestry incarcerated during World War II; and it awarded $20,000 each to over 80,000 Japanese Americans as reparations for their treatment. In his White House remarks, President Reagan noted, "We gather here today to right a grave wrong. This action was taken without trial or jury. It was based solely on race."

Sixteen years later, a different U.S. President, George W. Bush signed into law the Colorado River Indian Reservation Boundary Correction Act. This bill restored to the Colorado River Indian Tribes, "All right, title, and interest of the United States" to the 15,000 acres known as the La Paz lands that were stolen from them for the benefit of white ranchers and miners. It took 90 years to correct this injustice.

What the people of Harris Neck have been seeking is not a Presidential apology, reparations or a White House visit. They simply want some, if not all, of the lands taken from them in 1942. These are the lands the federal government repeatedly promised they would give back after World War II.

On September 30, 2012, California Governor Gavin Newsome signed into law a measure returning three acres of land to the descendants of Willa and Charles Bruce. In 1912, this black couple purchased this acreage in Manhattan

Beach, California. They built a successful resort destination known as Bruce's Beach that included ocean beach access, a bathhouse, musical entertainment and dining facilities. It was one of the few beach resorts available to blacks in southern California.

In 1924, the Manhattan Beach City Council used its eminent domain authority to condemn this property. The stated purpose was to build a public park but the real reason behind the taking was racism. The Bruce's land was taken in the same manner, as was Harris Neck.

On the day the legislation was signed into law, former Congresswoman and now Los Angeles County Supervisor Janice Hahn noted, "The law was used to steal this property 100 years ago, and the law today will give it back." It took nearly a century to correct this injustice. The current value of this property is estimated at $75 million dollars.

Sadly, the seizure of private land in the United States is not unusual. In fact, it has occurred far too often in marginalized communities. There is no statute of limitations on correcting an injustice or keeping promises. Every government makes mistakes. Our history is replete with them. The important thing is the willingness to correct them. The people of Harris Neck are still waiting.

According to the U.S. Fish and Wildlife Service, as of October 1984, 43,934 acres of land had been acquired through the condemnation efforts of the U.S. Department of Defense. This property was located in 11 states and Puerto Rico. It has been incorporated within 17 national wildlife refuges and one wildlife management area. None of these lands, except for Harris Neck, involved the taking of property from the descendants of former slaves.

Why is the Harris Neck National Wildlife Refuge important? Is it really needed? Congressman Bo Ginn, who proposed allowing the descendants to repurchase their land, noted, "Harris Neck is so close to Blackbeard (NWR) and some of the other islands involved, I simply do not believe that would be doing any irreparable damage to remove the refuge." Former Interior Secretary James

Watt famously said, "The equities are with the community, the land should be returned to them." Even, longtime FWS Savannah Project Leader John Potter Davis had to admit that the wildlife would not die from trauma if the land reverted to the original Harris Neck community.

As someone who has visited dozens of wildlife refuges throughout the United States, I can categorically state there is nothing unique or vitally important about these Harris Neck lands. Even FWS has largely abandoned the refuge. The visitor contact station has been closed for years. The wood storks were there long before the refuge was established, and they would survive just fine if land thousands of feet from their nesting sites were given back to the rightful owners.

Under the Gullah Geechee culture, there is a sacred environmental ethic to protect wildlife. In addition, the strong community covenants the Trust has written will ensure that this community would preserve Harris Neck's fauna and flora.

Over the past several decades, Harris Neck elders and descendants have worked tirelessly to correct this blatant injustice. They first sought relief in the courts and were summarily denied. They were told they couldn't get their lands back because time had run out and the actions of the federal government were sacrosanct.

They demonstrated and erected a tent city on their former lands within the Harris Neck National Wildlife Refuge. While they received favorable press coverage, they got no support from their former Governor, then President, Jimmy Carter. Instead, heavily armed U.S. Marshalls dragged four of the justice warriors off to jail.

During this same period, they were successful in persuading their locally elected Congressman, Bo Ginn, to introduce legislation on their behalf. They even got to testify in the People's House, and for the first time they had the chance to articulate how badly their government had treated them.

Sadly, a Congressional hearing was the high water mark in their efforts to achieve a legislative solution. We will never know what happened behind closed doors. Was Congressman Ginn unwilling to spend political capital to move this bill forward? Did the leadership of the House Merchant Marine and Fisheries Committee, who were all Democrats, tell him they lacked the votes to approve his proposal? What we do know is that the Carter Administration through the U.S. Fish and Wildlife Service strongly opposed the bill. How do we know this? Because if they supported the bill, it would have moved through the legislative process. You need to only remember the words of the FWS Realty Chief, "The Interior Department has no plans to return the wildlife property to the people who once lived there."

Since 1980, no legislation has been introduced to provide any relief to the descendants of Harris Neck. While there have been various conversations about a "new bill;" nothing has yet materialized. At this time, a legislative solution is going to be difficult, if not impossible, to achieve.

In fact, the introduction of a new bill would attract fanfare but also provide false hope to the community. The atmosphere within today's U.S. Congress is so toxic that it is difficult to pass any bill. Since it is highly unlikely the U.S. Congressman representing McIntosh County will propose or even vote for a legislative solution, the burden falls on Georgia's two U.S. Senators, Jon Ossoff and Raphael Warnock. If one of them were to introduce legislation it would be referred to the Senate Environment and Public Works Committee now Chaired by Senator Thomas Carper of Delaware.

If the sponsor were successful in getting a hearing on the bill, the Committee would hear from an array of organizations opposing it. Leading the charge would be the FWS. I would predict their testimony would be an updated version of the December 15, 2011 statement of then Regional Director Cynthia Dohner.

Fish and Wildlife officials would likely testify that they are very sorry about any past mistreatment, they are unaware of any inequities, they have no DOD records, the U.S. War Department was responsible for creating this issue (not FWS) and the Harris Neck National Wildlife Refuge is critical to the survival of the entire refuge system. The usual suspects of the Friends of the Savannah Coastal Wildlife Refuges, The National Audubon Society, the National Wildlife Refuge Association, The Nature Conservancy and the Sierra Club would join them in this opposition effort. It is not hard to imagine these groups convincing one or more U.S. Senators to stop any Harris Neck bill from moving forward.

After the FWS made it clear that it would never allow houses to be built on the refuge and Congressman Kingston advised against pursuing a legislative solution, the Trust abandoned its quest for title. Over the next several years, the Trust made various innovative and comprehensive proposals to the FWS. The Service denied each and every one.

The Trust applied to the FWS, for a Special Use Permit. Under Title 50, Subchapter C, Subpart F: Concessions, are "businesses operated by private enterprises that provide recreational, education and interpretative opportunities for the visiting public" are eligible for Special Use Permits.

Under their innovative proposal, the Trust would obtain a long-term lease on about 200 acres on the eastern side of the refuge. Upon these lands, they would build a living history museum, seafood and farmers' market, Gullah café, oyster house museum and a small number of guest cottages. These facilities would have provided a small semblance of justice and good jobs. They would have greatly enhanced the refuge visitor experience. And, for the first time, the story and struggles of those living in Harris Neck prior to 1942 would have been told. In addition, nutritional products and tasty seafood would have been available. Except for the wood storks, there is little, if any, reason to visit the current refuge. These modest improvements would have been overwhelmingly popular and would make the refuge a destination point.

Despite the fact that the leased lands represented a tiny portion of the entire refuge, then Refuge Manager Kimberly Hayes denied the Land Trust's Special Use Permit Application. In her March 31, 2015 response to Harris Neck Board Chair, Chester Dunham, Kimberly Hayes stated, "We have found that the proposed use of leasing refuge land to construct and develop residential, cultural and commercial areas does not meet the criteria of an appropriate use on a national wildlife refuge."

There were a number of problems with this letter. For instance, what is an appropriate use? The letter doesn't say. What if the Harris Neck Land Trust decided to only build cultural facilities like the Living Museum? Is this an appropriate use? There is no guidance provided and, who is the "We have found?" Why did the Regional Director of FWS in Atlanta or the FWS Director in Washington, D.C. not sign this letter, an idea that even Cynthia Dohner liked? Finally, Hayes statement says, "Any lease would impair existing wildlife dependent recreational opportunities." This is completely fallacious and even laughable.

The application covered a small amount of the refuge and would have no impact on recreational opportunities or wildlife.

Despite this setback, the Trust was not going to give up. Their next approach was a December 2018 Cooperative Agreement. In this proposal, the Harris Neck Community for Justice and Preservation, a non-profit organization that was established by the Trust in 2018, asked for a 25-year, renewable lease on about 500 acres. Upon this property, you would have key facilities such as a Gullah Geechee Café, Living Museum and visitor cottages. Of these 500 acres, less than 20 acres or .07 percent of the entire refuge would be developed. This comprehensive Cooperative Agreement would be of great historical and spiritual importance to the descendants of Harris Neck.

On January 14, 2020, Refuge Manager Kimberly Hayes, who was then located in Savannah, responded to the Harris Neck Land Trust Chair, Winston Relaford. In her letter, she stated, "The proposed use is considered a general public use that is not a wildlife-dependent recreational use and would not contribute to the fulfillment of refuge purposes, goals, or objectives."

What only a few people in this country know is that 155 of the 575 national wildlife refuges have had oil and gas exploration on them since the 1920s. There are nearly 2,000 active wells within 36 national wildlife refuges providing nearly a billion dollars in oil and gas resources. There are also 36 refuges with pipelines. These activities are not wildlife-dependent. Hundreds of oil spills have occurred within these refuge lands and yet these oil and gas activities still continue on hundreds of acres of federal property.

Another path that has been presented by FWS persistently to an uninterested Trust is the idea of a Land Exchange. If successfully negotiated in the case of Harris Neck, it could give the Trust ownership of a number of acres in the Harris Neck refuge. However, while FWS has undertaken land exchanges throughout the United States, the price is usually extraordinarily high and the time to complete them is measured in years.

During my Congressional career, I was involved in one of the most famous land exchanges involving the Izembek National Wildlife Refuge in Alaska. My boss, Chairman Don Young, represented the Alaskan Aleut community of King Cove, Alaska. This community had a population of about 965 people. For decades, the residents of this community would die from a lack of timely and proper medical care because their local airport was too small, dangerously close to high mountains and frequently closed because of bad weather. The solution was to convince FWS to finish building a one-lane gravel road to the community of Cold Bay, Alaska. Sadly, the community was consistently denied the opportunity to use Cold Bay's 10,000-foot all-weather runway.

Finally, in 2019, the Trump Administration negotiated a land exchange agreement. The price was staggering. In return for removing 206 acres from the Izembek refuge, FWS received 56,393 acres from the State of Alaska and the King Cove Corporation. Alaskans were willing to pay this steep price to save human lives who were going to be transported from Cold Bay to Anchorage, Alaska or Seattle, Washington.

Just one year later, a federal judge stopped the land exchange. On March 12, 2022, the Ninth Circuit Court of Appeals issued a ruling overturning the lower court's decision and allowing the exchange to go forward. At that time, the Congressman for all of Alaska, Don Young, who had worked on finding a solution for many years, said, "The proposed single-lane gravel road enjoys bipartisan support across two Administrations for good reason: in the event of medical emergencies, natural disasters or other crisis, access to surface transportation can mean the difference between life and death for residents of King Cove."

It was not surprising this land exchange was passionately opposed by many of the same groups who have rejected justice for Harris Neck. These organizations included: Friends of Alaska National Wildlife Refuges, National Wildlife Refuge Association and the Sierra Club. The land required for the road was less than 1 percent of the total refuge. These groups were willing to allow more native Alaskans to die then remove one inch of Izembek refuge land.

In terms of the Harris Neck Land Trust, even if the people were willing to sell their own neighboring homes, there isn't enough land or financial resources to pay what would be an obscene price. And in addition to the great cost, the idea itself was abhorrent to members of the Trust. The net effect would be they would have to buy their way back home. A land exchange was never going to work in Harris Neck.

It is our humble opinion the only viable solution to correcting this injustice is for the President of the United States to issue an Executive Order, removing a portion of the Harris Neck National Wildlife Refuge and returning it to the rightful descendants. Since the establishment of this Republic, every Chief Executive, except for William Henry Harrison, has issued Executive Orders. Some of the most important in our history are: The Emancipation Proclamation, Desegregation of the U.S. military, National Guard Deployment to Desegregate Public Schools and the

Creation of the Peace Corps. Since the establishment of the National Wildlife Refuge System, hundreds of units have been created by Presidential Executive Orders. Why can't one be issued to slightly alter an existing refuge?

Since becoming President, Joe Biden, as of this writing, has issued 102 Executive Orders. His very first one was to advance racial equity. A second established a Task Force for the Reunification of families. It is time to reunite the Harris Neck descendants whose ancestors sacrificed so much for this country. The days of making false promises must end.

With your signature, Mr. President, you can finally end over 80 years of suffering and pain. This action will cost U.S. taxpayers nothing. In fact, it would help McIntosh County, which desperately needs the ad valorem taxes that would be generated by removing lands from the refuge system. For the descendants of Harris Neck, it would mean everything.

The U.S. federal government has an obligation to keep its promises. Mr.

President, do the right thing. Issue the Executive Order. Let the people of Harris Neck, finally, realize their lifelong dream of Going Back Home.

AFTERWORD

JUSTICE. What a lovely word, a wonderful word. The sweet spoken sound of it, its balanced look on the page. For those who have been through exceptional struggles, it provokes a visceral response, and I think it fair to say that most, if not all, of us have been angered, even outraged, at injustices we have witnessed or personally experienced.

Justice is the principle of dealing fairly, rightly, correctly, and reasonably. It is the ideal behind every significant social movement in American history. Cornell West said, "Justice is what love looks like in public." Arnold Toynbe said, "The only real struggle in the history of the world - is between vested interest and justice." And L. E. Modesitt said, "Never mistake law for justice. Justice is an ideal; law is a tool."

The Constitution of the United States of America was written or "ordained" for six reasons, all of which are stated in the one-sentence Preamble to the Constitution. The first reason was to "form a more perfect Union." The second was to "establish Justice." The other four reasons are all important but the founding fathers got the order of the first two wrong, for you cannot have a perfect union without justice. Justice is the foundation. There can be nothing before or beneath it. It is the ideal that any society, which envisions itself as America does, must not only strive toward but be built upon. When there is no justice, there can be no equality, no liberty, no peace, and no strong union.

Justice has been so long-delayed for the people of Harris Neck that it has been denied them. Eighty years is four generations. It is three years longer than the people who lived on Harris Neck did so as free men and women.

America is not the country its most important document says it is. It is not a country where all people are treated equally, where all have their liberty, where there is real peace. No reasonable person, who does not live in a cave in the middle of some American wilderness, can disagree with this fact. However, it most certainly could be the America that appears on paper in the Constitution with its twenty-seven Amendments. It could be a country where the tools of its laws and its ideal of justice are one in the same. Men created this nation; men and women, can see to it that it becomes what it was supposed to be, what we are taught it is in elementary school.

And this "becoming" is not rocket science. It is not as difficult as it was to put a man on the moon or send spacecraft to search throughout the heavens. It is simply a matter of will and compassion and courage. However, to make this becoming a reality, we must first go back to our nation's foundation. The powerful writer and speaker, James Baldwin said that America would never become the society it could be until it makes amends for its two greatest sins – the genocide of its Indigenous Peoples and slavery. That is the part of our foundation that must be repaired.

Why has this repair not been made long ago? The reasons are the same reasons the people of Harris Neck have waited so long for restorative justice to come to them. They are three --- racism, bureaucracy and fear.

I have witnessed racism in different forms since my early childhood and have been aware of bureaucracy since, I suppose, my adult life began, perhaps somewhat earlier. However, I had never experienced the insidious nature of both of these evils until I moved to McIntosh County and became intimately involved in the Harris Neck Justice Movement.

Contemplating these two evils, I think what they have in common are their impersonal and systemic characteristics, and when human nature, with all its failings and weaknesses, naturally comes into the mix, terrible cruelty and suffering often result. Enslaved Americans, from the start, were thought of and treated so impersonally that the Constitution did not even consider them fully human, and when slavery soon became institutionalized in America all bets were off.

When human beings can be treated as things, or at least as chattel, and when that treatment is then systematized, then the most inconceivable can and, did happen. It happened in the summer of 1942 to the people of Harris Neck, and for the next 80 years – right up to the to the writing of this book – it has continued happening to them and their descendants.

Bureaucracy and, yes, racism are so deeply engrained in the federal agencies where the Harris Neck Land Trust still seeks justice that it is not all that surprising to me (though it is utterly disheartening for the people of Harris Neck) that justice is still being denied them.

Many laws attempting to eliminate injustice have been passed in America, yet this nation remains deeply affected by its past, which as Faulkner said is "never dead ... not even past." But, as Modesitt reminds us, laws are just tools; they should not be mistaken for justice. So, where do these realities leave us with regard to the terrible damage that systemic racism still inflicts on our society and still leaves so many as second class citizens? Where do we go from here? This is where fear, the third reason for Harris Neck's unresolved limbo, comes into the equation for continued injustice.

The fear of those in Congress and other positions of power to take a stand on this issue shows how deeply America still lives in its past. I have personally witnessed this fear – with every single person in power who could have made (and some who still can make) a difference for the people of Harris Neck.

But there can only be one valuable and honorable response to these specific fears, just as there can only be one positive response to fear in general. We must all – every day and in every way – do the right thing, the correct thing, the just thing. We must. If we do not, we continue living in the past, which, for so many Americans, was, and still is, a horrible, dangerous, life-threatening place to live.

Will, compassion and courage. All three are needed to achieve an equitable resolution for Harris Neck, just as all three are needed in every single step this nation must take to make America what it could be and to save its very soul, because losing that soul is just what is happening now. The evidence is all around us. Our present danger is our past danger. The picture is as clear as it can be.

For everyone not living somewhere in a

cave, our reality is clear. We can deny that reality, or we can look straight at it, frightening, at first, as that may be. And then we can act and do so courageously, and in the process truly become the land of the free and home of the brave.

David M. Kelly
Fall 2022

ACKNOWLEDGMENTS

December 15, 2011, was a seminal moment in my Congressional career. Over the course of eight different Congresses, I was responsible for the planning and execution of 278 legislative and oversight hearings. What I heard at the oversight hearing on Harris Neck, Georgia changed my life. I first wrote about the injustice that occurred in that small rural Georgia community in 2016 with the publication of *The National Wildlife Refuge System: History, Laws and Abuses of Power.*

Without the eloquence and deeply moving testimony of Wilson W. Moran, Reverend Robert H. Thorpe, Evelyn Greer, Winston B. Relaford Sr. and David M. Kelly, I would never have heard about Harris Neck and neither the 1996 chapter or this new book would ever have been written. I am, therefore, deeply grateful to all the members of the Harris Neck Land Trust.

I also want to acknowledge the invaluable assistance of Professor Autumn Johnson at Georgia Southern

University for providing me with some important documents and the members of my Marshall Writing Group, Annette Lewis, Anita Metzger, Linda Moore and Joy Schaya.

This book would not have been published without the counsel, patience and understanding of my beautiful wife, Gayle. We have built a wonderful life with our sons Rick and Chris, their wives Erin and Stacey and our precious grandchildren Mitchell, Elise, Kelly, Christopher and Connor.

A heartfelt thanks to my remarkable dear friend Joy Schaya, who spent many hours reading, editing and improving this book. Joy is an outstanding writer of children's and young adult books. To my son Chris, I may write the words but he is responsible for ensuring people have the opportunity to read them. Thank you for making me look good.

Finally, I want to acknowledge the lifelong commitment to justice of Wilson Moran. His forward to this book is deeply moving and highly personal. To my friend and co-writer, Dave Kelly, thank you for your willingness to join me in telling this important story. It had to be told and justice must prevail. Your contributions were enormous and your willingness to move from California to Georgia to fight for this righteous cause was admirable and noble.

The front cover of this book includes a picture of Rev. Robert H. Thorpe, the First Chair of the Harris Neck Land Trust, saying a prayer at the beginning of a meeting with the Regional Director of the U. S. Fish and Wildlife Service, Cynthia Dohner and her staff and members of the Harris Neck Land Trust community. A second image is of Wilson Moran, his mother, Mary Dawley Moran and Samuel Beetler II. Samuel is the coordinator for the City of Savannah's Department of Cemeteries Conservation and the artist of the Robert Dawley house.

The back cover is Harris Neck protesters outside the FWS Refuge during Secretary Sally Jewell's visit June 2014. (Image provided by the Darien News, Darien, Georgia).

EXHIBITS

The Uniqueness of Harris Neck

The uniqueness of Harris Neck lies in the culture and the history of Harris Neck and the people's relationship with the land and waters of this community. In September 1865, Margret Ann Harris deeded her 2,687-acre coastal planation, "Harris Neck," to her former slave Robert Delegall. This transfer of property established rightful ownership of the land to former African American slaves. Harris Neck grew to 75 families who established a peaceful subsistence fishing and farming community that thrived on this land for 77 years from 1865 to 1942.

The Harris Neck community was a unique example of a Gullah Geechee settlement. This proud ethnic group carried on the traditions of West Africa and integrated them into a thriving subsistence existence in the coastal regions of Georgia and South Carolina. The Gullah Geechee communities have a distinct language, culture and spirituality, and, by retaining many African traditions represent the most intact West African culture in the United States today.

In 2006, the United States Congress approved the Gullah Geechee Cultural Heritage Corridor Act. This important legislation recognized the cultural and historical importance of the Gullah Geechee people. It provide funding to preserve historical sites in North and South Carolina and northern Florida relating to Gullah culture to be administered by the National Park Service.

The families descending from the Harris Neck Gullah Geechee community have continued their connection to Harris Neck. In order to maintain a connection to their homeland, many of the descendant families still live along Harris Neck Road, adjacent to the Harris Neck National Wildlife Refuge.

Based on data presented to the Congress by a 1985 General Accounting Office Report, the way in which the Harris Neck property was incorporated within the refuge system --- through the transfer of surplus Department of Defense land that had been originally been condemned is unlike 99.95 percent of all land comprising the National Wildlife Refuge System. This was a unique acquisition. No other refuge property owned by former slaves and their dependents has been added in this manner.

Furthermore, the circumstances surrounding the Harris Neck condemnation, at a time in U.S. history, when racial bias and discrimination was much more prevalent than today, raises issues of both substantive and procedural inequity. Finally, limited human habitation on Harris Neck lands would be managed consistent with conservation values. While living on the land, Harris Neck residents were proud of their long tradition of conserving and protecting wildlife.

Harris Neck is a combination of lands that are unique throughout the National Wildlife Refuge System. The federal government promised the people of Harris Neck that they would get their property back after World War II. They are still waiting for the government to honor its commitment to this unique community.

CONGRESSIONAL TESTIMONY
COMMITTEE ON NATURAL RESOURCES
U.S. HOUSE OF REPRESENTATIVES
DECEMBER 15, 2011

Wilson W. Moran
Board Member
Harris Neck Land Trust LLC
12/12/2011

It really started for us in 1863. General William Sherman issued Field Order 15, giving us ownership of all the islands starting from the southern tip of North Carolina, through South Carolina, Georgia and to the northern tip of Florida. Including some land up to 30 miles inland on the mainland. My great grandfather Mustapha D. Shaw son of Edward Delegal, a white land owner, having been injured while fighting in the Union Army, jumped at the opportunity to own land. Owning land was a form of freedom. He went to live on Ossabaw Island, just southeast of Savannah, GA. He did well utilizing his skills as a farmer and fisherman but it was short lived as President Lincoln was assassinated during this period in Mustapha's life. President Johnson became the new President. The power people convinced President Johnson to rescind Field Order 15. Thus my people lost everything. My grandfather refused to become a sharecropper.

A warrant was issued for his arrest. Armed with his army issued Revolver, Rifle and Bowie knife, he fought his way off Ossabaw Island, got into a boat and disappeared. He escaped to his grandfather's old plantation which was situated near Harris Neck. Once again he was back to zero. Then another strange thing happened. Margaret Harris, an heir, was given ownership of most of the old plantation homes. She was elderly and her son was mentally ill. Because her white overseers were cheating her, she employed a black man, Robert Delegall to be her overseer. She made a will and testament. In this Will, Robert would agree to take care of her and her son. In turn he could sell land to the black people already living on said property. Eventually, Robert sold most of the land to about 75 black families. Now we have to start again. By the late 1S00's, we are doing extremely well.

We have a church house, firehouse, school house, crab factory and oyster factory. We are buying and selling. We are quickly learning that freedom is closely tied to economics. After much blood, sweat and tears we are beginning to reap some of the benefits of our hard labor. After many years of hopelessness we now have hope. In 1942 it happened again. It's World War II and the German U-Boats are blowing up our merchant ships. The war department needed a place in which to build an airbase. Our white county leaders steered them to the community of Harris Neck. Our government claimed Imminent Domain, giving us two weeks to move out. In a blink of an eye, we were wiped out. We lost everything, including our culture. Now we are back to zero again.

Rev. Robert H. Thorpe
Former Board Chairman of the
Harris Neck Land Trust and Harris Neck
Elder

I was born on Harris Neck April 3rd 1931 in this house, where I was raised by my grandparents, Robert and Amelia Dawley. In 1942 the Federal government sent surveyors in to Harris Neck to survey our land without any notice or questions, and about a week after they sent in a government representative from Washington, DC whose name was Mr. Banks. Mr. Banks came to our house, and my grandfather went out and spoke with him and I went along. Mr. Banks said he represented the Federal government and that the government needed our property for an army airbase, and that we would have to move out in a few days. Then my grandfather asked him, "If you take our property are we going to get it back?" And Mr. Banks said, "Yes, when the government is finished with it they will return it back to you. My grandfather asked him, "If we have to move where should we go?" He said: "I don't know anything about that. All I know is you have to move in a few days, and if you don't move your house and everything will be destroyed - pushed down or burned." So, my grandfather asked him if we were going to get any help for moving. He said, "No, you'll have to move on your own."

So, my grandfather took his crowbar and hammer and went to the front door first and started taking the facing off the door. And piece by piece he tried to save all the lumber on the house, because he had no money to buy materials to build another house at that time or to move. At that time our crops were just maturing, and we had to leave all that behind us. And that was part of our living. Com, potatoes, beans, tomatoes, all our fruit and nut trees. All that was left behind and destroyed.

We were offered a piece of land a couple of miles away by Mr. Irvin Davis of McIntosh County. We had to purchase this land, which was in Eagle Neck, from Mr. Davis. It was an acre and a half, much less than what we had on Harris Neck. We planted a small garden, which again was nothing like what we had on Harris Neck. After the war ended, the same Irvin Davis came out to our church, First African Baptist - which we had taken down on Harris Neck and rebuilt on Eagle Neck - with his lawyer who spoke for him.
He told us that the government is not using the land anymore now, but they're not going to return it back to us right yet. He asked us if we would agree to let Mr. Davis use the land as a cow pasture for his cows. We said, "Yes, Mr. Davis is welcome to use the land." It was years later that we found out that the Federal

358

government had given the land to McIntosh County. We never knew anything about any proceedings that had taken place between the Federal government and the county about this.

Then again, years after that, we found out that the Federal government had taken the land back from the county and again, without our knowledge or any word from the government or anyone else, it gave the land, this time, to Fish and Wildlife.

Justice for us from Harris Neck can only come from the return of our land. However, we have offered Fish and Wildlife to be partners with us in the new Harris Neck community. We would like them to continue doing their job of monitoring the ponds and protecting wildlife, which we will be setting aside and protecting in our plans. But we feel it is only just that our land be returned to us.

Testimony of Evelyn Greer
Residents of Harris Neck Community in 1942
Member of Harris Neck Land Trust, and
Harris Neck Elder

Good morning. My name is Evelyn Greer. And I...Just want to say, this afternoon, to you all, that I'm 84 years old. I was 15 when the government took my home, and I told them They told us, as Reverend Thorpe said, (unintelligible). I was there. We didn't get no kind of compensation. Please believe it. None. My home burned, and everything I saw. There was no place to go, you know. So I just I was trying to get some time,

but my, I got so anyhow, I just want to say that it is time now, as he said, for justice. We are here today not as beggars. We are here to see and ask you all to let justice prevail. We need the property. God made arrangement for the birds and the bees, but he said the son of man has no place to lay his head. And we thank you.

Testimony of Winston B. Relaford, Sr.
Vice Chairman of the Harris Neck Land Trust

I am Winston Relaford the son of Anna Shaw Overstreet, a descendant of the original Harris Neck community. My appearance before this august body today has one goal; and that is to plea to this committee to correct and obvious wrong. I appeal to you today to ensure that history correctly record and reflect a Congress that dared to do the right thing by upholding the constitutional rights of all of its citizens.

What was done to the Harris Neck community in 1942 was an injustice or wrong that must be righted and this committee has within its power to move on behalf of a neglected portion of America's citizenry. Let history show that you stood up today and began the process of making right, an awful wrong. As you ponder the right and wrong, please remember the humanity of it all. You have heard the testimony of an impassioned and embattled people ask of a government to honor them as they honored the government by giving in to demands that turned out to be way to costly. Our forefathers trusted the government because they loved this country and wanted it to succeed against our foreign enemies, but little did they know that the enemy from within posed a far greater threat to their constitutional rights and freedoms than that of a government that betrayed their trust.

In closing, I simply ask on behalf of the families that were displaced so long ago that you return the land back to its rightful owners and they are the descendants of the Harris Neck people. To this committee, may God bless each of you and may God bless the United States of America.

Testimony of David M. Kelly

Project Coordinator, Harris Neck Land Trust

Honorable members of this subcommittee and others who may be in attendance at this hearing, we thank you for your invitation to testify before you on December 15, 2011. We would also like to thank our Representative, Congressman Jack Kingston, for all the support and advice he has provided us during the six years of the Harris Neck Justice Movement.

I will speak to the following issues that we were asked to address in your December 7, 2011 letter of invitation.

1. A brief history of how the Federal government obtained Harris Neck.
2. How were the owners compensated?
3. Whether assurances were given that the community could reclaim the property.
4. What steps have been taken by the Federal government and community to address this issue during the past 70 years?
5. Has the Federal government offered to compensate anyone represented by the Harris Neck Land Trust?

I am sure we have all heard the expression "Speak truth to power". Well, we from• Harris Neck, wish to speak truth to misinformation, misconception, inaccurate statements, rumor, and outright lies that have been, and continue being, spread about the Harris Neck Land Trust and our plans for a new Harris Neck community. We, respectfully, come before this subcommittee to set the record straight about Harris Neck. In that regard I will address five issues listed in your December 7th letter, one by one, and make some additional relevant comments.

1.   The history of the taking of Harris Neck:
     The taking of Harris Neck - located in northeast McIntosh County, on the coast of Georgia some 40 miles south of Savannah -

in 1942 occurred because of a conspiracy among McIntosh County officials who intentionally led representatives of the Federal government to Harris Neck, right past more than 3,500 acres of virtually uninhabited land, just a good stones throw from the southwest border of the community. This other available property had been owned by E. M. Thorpe, one of the largest landowners, at that time, in McIntosh County. According to many families in Harris Neck, E. M. Thorpe had acquired much of his property in Harris Neck by underhanded and unethical practices, and by the time of the taking in 1942, he was the largest landowner in Harris Neck - white or black.

The original taking via Eminent Domain was highly illegal, with the people's Fifth Amendment rights to Due Process being violated in a number of ways through its hurried and carelessly executed implementation of Eminent Domain. A list of these violations is being submitted with this testimony.

1.   Compensation: The key word in the law, regarding compensation, is that it be "just". The taking of Harris Neck was not just, not by a long measure, because first, not everyone was paid. Second, white families, who owned property but did not live on Harris Neck and had not made any improvements to their property (with the

exception of the two single white women who lived in the community), were paid 40 percent more than the African American families who, over the decades since the end of the Civil War, had created a thriving community with houses, barns, other out-buildings, seafood processing buildings, general store, churches and more. Third, not a single African American family was paid for anything but their property; there were no payments for any "improvements" as required under Eminent Domain. Fourth, payments from the Federal government did not go directly to the African American families; they went through E. M. Thorpe, who may or may not have disbursed monies correctly and fairly.

E.M. Thorpe <u>may</u> have been designated as an agent for these Harris Neck transactions by the government, but he was no friend of the people from Harris Neck. Rev. Thorpe and Wilson Moran will speak better and more personally to this.

2.   <u>Assurances to the community about reclaiming its property:</u> Reverend Thorpe will speak more personally to this. However, regarding assurances or a promise made to return the property after World War II, I would like to site the 1934 decision of *Olson v. United States.* In this case it was rightly stated that the owner of condemned property should be placed *"in as good a position pecuniarily as if his*

property had not been taken. He must be made
whole, but is not entitled to more. It is the
property and not the cost of it that is
safeguarded by state and federal constitutions."
The community was destroyed. Their entire
way of life - their livelihood - was destroyed.
People died heartbroken months later. The
people were greatly harmed and left in a much-
worse-off position than they were before the
taking.

It was the Federal government's
responsibility after World War II to contact
members of the former Harris Neck
community, whether or not there was a
promise to return the land, which all the
living elders will swear to the fact that there
was, indeed, such a promise made. Many
families from Harris Neck were then (after the
war) living within two miles of their
homeland; they stayed close by because of
what they had been told by the government:
Don't go far; the land will be returned to you
after the war. However, after the war the
government talked only with McIntosh
County officials, and even though the county
commission did some good public talking, at
that time, about reacquiring the land on
behalf of the former community members, the
county got the land for itself in 1947.

Over the next 14 years, county officials used
Harris Neck for a number of illegal ventures -
including prostitution, gambling and drug
smuggling - while the contract with the War

Assets Administration said the land was to be used only for a county airport. But this was how things went in the I940s in McIntosh and neighboring counties. This section of Georgia was run by what was referred to as the "Big Four", a small group of corrupt and very powerful men that included the infamous McIntosh County Sheriff Tom Poppell. To deny the reality of life for

African Americans in this region in 1942 or not to consider it in this matter creates an opening for continuing injustice.
Because of all the county's abuses of its contract, the Federal government took the land back in 1961. It then had another chance to bring justice to Harris Neck, but instead it once again did not contact anyone from Harris Neck and chose, instead, to transfer title to the Department of Interior. Since 1962, the United States Fish and Wildlife Service (FWS) has used Harris Neck as a National Wildlife Refuge.

In both instances (after the war and in 1961-62) no one from Harris Neck knew anything about official proceedings regarding their property until well after the deals were done and the property was in the hands of McIntosh County and FWS, respectively.

It does not matter how FWS came to be titleholder of Harris Neck or that, as personnel from FWS have told us, they are just carrying out their mission as mandated by law. What matters is that the original taking was wrong and it was illegal, and, therefore, we contend, each transfer of title since the original taking has been invalid and, therefore the property still belongs to the original families.

   4.   Steps taken over the past 70 years to address this issue: The government has not initiated any such steps. The community has made them, starting in the late 1970's, and the government has responded. To speak briefly about the lawsuit that was filed on behalf of the people of Harris Neck and the decision rendered by Judge Avant Edenfield in 1980, both are irrelevant today, since there was never any legal remedy available to Harris Neck; justice (equity) lies only with Congress. And as Congress showed in 2005, when it legislated the return of more than 15,000 acres to the Colorado River Indian Tribes (CRIT), there is no statute of limitations on justice, thus speaking to Judge Edenfield's main point in his decision - that, by 1980, too much time had passed on this issue. (CRIT's land was taken before Harris Neck was taken - during Woodrow Wilson's presidency.) And on the issue of equity, I would like to state that everyone from Judge Edenfield to Secretary of Interior James Watt has said that the equity with regard to Harris Neck belongs with the community, not the government. There was also legislation drafted in this time period, but due to lack of support, H.R.4018 never made it out of committee.

Nothing much happened, regarding the property, from the early 1980s until 2006, when community representatives first met with Congressman Jack Kingston to speak about the issue of Eminent Domain and other concerns. Since then, representatives of the Harris Neck Land Trust, which was formed in 2006, have been working with Mr. Kingston and several other members of Congress. In December 2009 we met with Mr. Kingston, Congressman John Lewis, legislative staff of other congressmen, and high-ranking officials of FWS. At that meeting, everyone in Congressman Kingston's office agreed to find what Mr. Kingston called for - an "equitable solution" to this issue. In March of 2010 we had a follow-up meeting, with most of the same parties in attendance, at the Savannah regional headquarters office of FWS. A few months later Board Chair, Rev. Robert Thorpe received a letter from FWS, offering us 1) a homecoming day and 2) a kiosk. This is FWS's idea of an equitable solution.

We have dealt honestly and openly with everyone involved during the past six years of the Harris Neck Justice Movement, but we do not feel FWS has acted honestly or professionally. For example, at the March 2010 meeting a FWS archeologist said that another reason the land could not be returned to the people is that Harris Neck is "wall-to-wall" archeological/cultural sites.

The scientific literature shows that there are only a handful of such sites. (Please see our map, being submitted, of these sites - north of Harris Neck Road.) We have met with one of the premier archeological/cultural resource management firms in the southeast, and we plan to have them conduct the first-ever, comprehensive, acre-by-acre site analysis. We will protect and preserve whatever is found, as well as the few presently identified sites, and we plan to sign these sites and make them part of one of our many educational programs in the new Harris Neck.

5. <u>The government's offer to compensate anyone represented by the Trust:</u> Aside from the kiosk and homecoming day that FWS has offered (mentioned above), the Federal government has not made any offer of compensation to any individual represented by the Harris Neck Land Trust. Regarding compensation, the Trust does not want any financial compensation; the Trust wants the land of Harris Neck (all 2,687 acres) to be returned to the rightful owners - the white and black families/individuals that owned property on Harris Neck in 1942.

SOURCES

Introduction

Letter to the Honorable Doc Hastings, Chairman, Committee on Natural Resources, From the Honorable Jack Kingston, First Congressional District in Georgia, Concerning Harris Neck, Georgia, October 2011.

Harris Neck: Chronology, Harris Neck Land Trust, www.harrisnecklandtrust. Org.

Hearing before the Subcommittee on Fisheries, Wildlife Conservation and the Environment, H.R. 4018, Harris Neck, Georgia, Committee on Merchant Marine and Fisheries Committee, U. S. House of Representatives, December 7, 1979, Serial Number: 96-27.

United States Constitution, Amendment V, 1791.

Chapter 1: Chains of Enslavement

Coulter, E. Merton, A List of Early Settlers of Georgia, *The University of Georgia Press,* 1949.

Jackson, Edwin, James Oglethorpe, *New Georgia Enclopedia,* July 31, 2020. www.GeorgiaEnclopedia.org.

Kiger, Patrick J, 8 Things We Know About Crispus Attucks, www.history.com.

Wax, Donald D, Georgia and the Negro Before the American Revolution, *The Georgia Historical Quartly,* Vol. 51, No. 1, March 1967.

Jennison, Watson W, Cultivating Race: The Expansion of Slavery in Georgia, 1750-1860, *The University of Kentucky Press,* 2012.

Oxgood, Herbert L, American Colonies in the Eighteenth Century, *Peter Smith Inc.,* April 1, 1865.

Kidd, Thomas S, George Whitefield's Troubled Relationship to Race and

Slavery, *The Christian Century,* January 6, 2015.

Dred Scott Case. November 4, 2019, www.history.com.

Kemble, Frances Anne, Journal of a Residence on a Georgia Plantation, 1838-1839, *Harper and Brothers Publishers,* 1863.

Kilmeade, Brian, The President and the Freedom Fighter, *Sentinel,* 2021.

Chapter 2: Origins of Harris Neck

Chauhan, Yamini, History of the War of Jenkins Ear, *Britannica,* July 23, 2010.

Sweet, Julie Ann, Battle of Bloody Marsh, *New Georgia Encyclopedia,* February 13, 2003.

Bhutia, Thinley Kalsang, The Crowning of King Cotton, *Britannica,* August 19, 2014.

Coastes, Ta-Nehisti, Slavery Made American. *The Atlantic,* June 14, 2014.

Kemble, Frances Anne, Journal of a Residence on a Georgia Plantation, 1838-1839, *Harper and Brothers Publishers,* 1863.

Martin, Susan, The Pretty Little Place Was Burnt to the Ground. The Destruction of Darien, Georgia, *The Beehive,* Massachusetts Historical Society, October 27, 2017.

Congressional Medal of Honor Society, William Harvey Carney, February 16, 2021, www.cmohs.org.

Charles River Editors, Sherman's March to the Sea, Civil War: ISO Pinhole Project.

Willis, Charles Wright, Army Life of an Illinois Soldier: Sherman's March to the Sea, *Globe Publishing Company,* 1906.

Chapter 3: Death of Slavery

Bruce, Henry Clay, The New Man: Twenty-Nine Years a Slave, Twenty-Nine Years a Free Man, *P.S. Anstadt and Sons,* 1895.

Grant, U.S, Personal Memoirs of U.S. Grant, Vol. II, *Charles L. Webster and Company,* 1886.

Reed, Annette Gordon, Andrew Johnson, *Times Books,* January 18, 2011.

Will and Testament of Margret Harris, Saint Catherine's Island, Georgia, September 2, 1865.

Opala, Joseph A, The Gullah: Rice, Slavery, and the Sierra Leone-American Connection: www.oglc.yale.edu.

Gullah/Geechee Cultural Heritage Act, U.S. House of Representatives, *The Congressional Record,* February 24, 2016.

History of Oystering in Georgia, From Harvest to Product, Georgia Coastal Resources Division, www.coastalgadnr.org.

H.R. 694, Gullah/Geeche Cultural Heritage Act, Public Law 109-338, October 12, 2006.

Drums and Shadows: Survival Studies
Amongst the Georgia Coastal Negroes,
Georgia Writer's Project, 1940.

Amelia's Song: A Song Led Them Home,
Harris Neck Land Trust,
www.harrisnecklandtrust.org.

Chapter 4: War Comes to Harris Neck

Elisha McDonald Thorpe, *The Desert
News,* March 1, 1966.

Russell, Kathleen, July 27, 1942
REMEMBERED: The Day of the "Taking"
of Harris Neck Land, *The Darien News,*
July 30, 2020.

Olson v. United States, U.S. Supreme
Court, 292: U.S. 246, April 30, 1934.

Ware, Catherine, Old Land Battle
Resurfaces in Georgia Between the Gullah
and the Government, *NPR,* March 18,
2015.

Thorpe, Robert H., Rev, Harris Neck: 70
Years to Justice, *Savannah Now,* July 26,
2012.

Freeman, Paul, Abandoned and Little-Known Airfields: Southeastern Georgia, 2002, www.airfields.freeman.com.

Rumerman, Judy, Airships and Balloons in the World War II Period, U.S. Centennial of Flights Commission.

Smith, Rocky, *Mr. Write's Page,* History Writ Small, February 27, 2011.

Chapter 5: Poppell's Playground

Thomas H. Poppell, *Brunswick News,* August 16, 1979.

Greene, Melissa Fay, Praying for Sheetrock, *Addison-Wesley Publishers Company, Inc.,* 1991.

Reid, Scotty, Return Harris Neck Land to Rightful Owners, Change.org.

Thousands of Tourists Fleeced on U.S. 17 in McIntosh County, *The Atlanta Journal.*

New National Wildlife Refuge Established on Atlantic Coast in Georgia, U.S. Fish and Wildlife Service, Press Release, June 13, 1962.

Harris Neck: The Story of Harris Neck, U.S. Fish and Wildlife Service, www.fws.gov.

Chini, Harris Neck Battles U.S. Government, *Southern Collection of African American Writers,* 1979.

Greene, Melissa Fay, The Old Man Who Led a Georgia County Into the 20th Century, *Los Angles Times,* December 15, 1991.

Special Harris Neck Program, *60 Minutes,* CBS News, February 20, 1983

Nunn, Sam, Mattingly, Mack and Thomas, Lindsay, Letter to Charles Bowsher, Comptroller General of the United States, July 24, 1984.

The Federal Government's 1943 Acquisition of Land at Harris Neck, Georgia, United States Government Accounting Office, May 29, 1985.

Chapter 6: Seeking A Solution

Evicted Colony Claims Wildlife Return in Georgia, *New York Times,*
May 1, 1979.

Prugh, Jeff, 4 Black Squatters Ejected From Georgia Wildlife Refuge, *Los Angles Times*, May 2, 1979.

Johnson, Thomas A, 4 Demonstrators Arrested at Georgia Wildlife Refuge, *New York Times*, May 3, 1979.

Johnson, Thomas A, 4 Blacks Are Sentenced to 30 Days in Dispute Over Refuge Ownership, *New York Times*, May 5, 1979.

Blacks Fight to Regain Land They "Lost" in 1942 in Harris Neck, GA., *Jet Magazine*, May 24, 1979.

Hearing before the Subcommittee on Fisheries, Wildlife Conservation and the Environment, H.R. 4018, Harris Neck, Georgia, Committee on Merchant Marine and Fisheries, U. S. House of Representatives, December 7, 1979, Serial Number: 96-27.

Office of U.S. Representative Bo Ginn, Harris Neck Legislation Press Release, May 9, 1979.

United States v. Timmons, United States Court of Appeals, Eleventh Circuit, April 12, 1982.

Harris Neck Army Airfield, McIntosh County, Georgia, Acquisition Data, U.S. War Department, 1980.

Osinski, Bill, Families Evicted by Army Claim McIntosh Refuge, *Atlanta Journal-Constitution,* March 17, 2002.

Jackson, Gordon, Residents Pushing on Land Dispute, *The Brunswick News,* September 6, 2012.

Landers, Mary, At Harris Neck, Struggle Continues for Land, *The Savannah Morning News,* February 5, 2014.

Morrison, Mike, Failing to Regain Land Taken in World War II, Harris Neck Descendants have Applied for Lease, *Jacksonville News,* February 8, 2015.

Chapter 7: Birth of Harris Neck Trust

National Public Radio, Living on Earth, 2000.

Margret Ann Harris' Will and Testament, Georgia Department of Archives and History.

Map of Harris Neck, Georgia, U. S. War Department, 1945.

Beirdsdort and Associates, Minneapolis, Minnesota.

McIntosh County Board of Commissioners, Resolution in Support of Harris Neck Justice Movement, 2006.

Chapter 8: Going to Washington

Dohner, Cynthia, Regional Director, U.S. Fish and Wildlife Service, U. S. Department of the Interior, Letter to Robert S. Highsmith, Jr., Executive Partner, Holland and Knight, October 17, 2013.

Dewan, Shaila, Black Landowners Fight to Reclaim Georgia Land, *New York Times,* July 1, 2010.

Phillips, Catherine, Black Landowners Prepare for Final Fight to Win Back

Thriving Society, *The London Times*, July 10, 2010.

Oversight Hearing on Harris Neck National Wildlife Refuge and How the Federal Government Obtained Title to This Land and Promises Made to the Original Landowners, Subcommittee on Fisheries, Wildlife, Oceans and Insular Affairs, Committee on Natural Resources, U.S. House of Representatives, December 15, 2011, Serial No. 112-2011.

Secretary Jewell to Announce Conservation Success Story at Georgia's Harris Neck National Wildlife Refuge, U. S. Department of the Interior, June 14, 2014.

Hayes, Kimberly, Refuge Manager, Fish and Wildlife Service, U. S. Department of the Interior, Letter to Chester Dunham, Harris Neck Land Trust, March 31, 2015.

Miranda-Castro, Leopoldo, Regional Director, Fish and Wildlife Service, U. S. Department of the Interior, Letter to Senator David A. Perdue, August 15, 2019.

Hayes, Kimberly, Refuge Manager, Fish and Wildlife Service, U.S. Department of the Interior, Letter to Winston Relaford, Harris Neck Community for Justice and Preservation, January 14, 2020.

Chapter 9: Still Searching

Oversight Hearing on Harris Neck National Wildlife Refuge and How the Federal Government Obtained Title to This Land and Promises Made to the Original Landowners, Subcommittee on Fisheries, Wildlife, Oceans and Insular Affairs, Committee on Natural Resources, U.S. House of Representatives, December 15, 2011, Serial No. 112-2011.

The Honorable John Fleming, (American Politician), Wikipedia, https://en.Wikipedia.org.

Refuge Revenue Sharing Act, 1935.

Annual Refuge Revenue Sharing Payment Summary by State and Local Governments, U.S. Fish and Wildlife Service, 2021.

McIntosh County Board of Assessors Office, Darien, Georgia, https://McIntosh Assessor. Com.

Chapter 10:

Will and Testament of Margret Harris, 1865.

Civil Liberties Act, P.L. 100-383, The White House, August 10, 1988.

Dazio, Stefanie, California Takes Step to Return Land to Black Couple's Heirs, *AP*, September 30, 2021.

FWS Refuge Lands Originally Acquired Through Condemnation by the Military as of October 1984.

Fletcher, Matthew L.M, Nine Circuit Approves Land Exchange over Enviros Objections to Allow King Cove Corp. to Build a Road through the Izembek National Wildlife Refuge, *Turtle Talk*, March 17, 2022.

Executive Orders, The American Presidency Project, *U C Santa Barbara*, 2022.

Crafton, R. Eliot, Oil and Gas Activities within the National Wildlife Refuge

System, *Congressional Research Service,* May 9, 2018.

Barton, Tom, Barton: End Harris Neck Injustice, *The Savannah Morning News,* April 19, 2009.

Harry Frederick Burroughs III was born in Riverhead, New York. He began his career in the United States House of Representatives on May 16, 1977. For the next 37 years, he worked for six members of Congress, served as Republican Chief of Staff of the House Merchant Marine and Fisheries Committee, and the Staff Director of the House Natural Resources Subcommittee on Fisheries, Wildlife, Oceans, and Insular Affairs.

Since retiring in 2015, Harry has written a number of books including *My Life on Capitol Hill, The National Wildlife Refuge System: History, Laws, and Abuses of Power and The Congressman For All of Alaska.* The author lives with his wife, Gayle, in Northern Virginia.

David Kelly is a writer and community organizer, who has been working on social and environmental justice issues for most of his career. Shortly after 9/11, he moved to McIntosh County, GA and has been involved in the fight for justice in Harris Neck since then. He is the Executive Director of the Harris Neck Land Trust.

This is the story of an isolated community in Georgia known as Harris Neck. Between 1865 and 1942, four generations of black Americans, descendants of slaves who had worked the same land and lived on the 2,687 acres of Harris Neck and the surrounding waters. In 1942, the U.S. Department of War wanted to construct an Army airfield on the Georgia coast to train fighter pilots for World War II. Federal officials met with McIntosh County, Georgia political leaders. Despite there being thousands of acres of suitable, undeveloped and even uninhabited land in the county, the War Department followed the racist advice of white county leaders and condemned all of Harris Neck.

Community residents were given three weeks to vacate their property. On July 27 1942, bulldozers arrived and destroyed everything --- their homes, businesses, schoolhouse and one of two cemeteries. Everything was then burned to the ground. Their community, their culture and their way of life were obliterated because of the color of their skin. Left completely homeless, residents were forced to seek refuge in an adjacent pine forest. They constructed lean-tos and set up tents to protect them from the stifling summer heat. According to community matriarch, Mary Dawley Moran, they were "treated like animals."

As they were building their new lives, their one hope was the promise made by the United States federal government that their land would be returned after the war. This solemn promise was never kept.

For over 80 years, the Harris Neck elders and their descendants have fought for justice. They have tried federal courts, the United States Congress and the Executive Branch, and for the past 16 years they have worked tirelessly with the Department of the Interior and the U. S. Fish and Wildlife Service. As of this writing, however, there has been no "equitable resolution" to the tragic reality of Harris Neck, but even at this late hour the people of Harris Neck have not given up. They are still striving and hoping and praying that Congress or the President will keep the promise they made to them eight decades ago. And while this is their fight, every American should be angry about this historical injustice and cry out for it to be corrected.

Made in the USA
Middletown, DE
04 November 2023